LETTERS TO THEOPHILUS

Are You Ready For The End Times?

SECOND EDITION

Dr. David Alan Greene

GraceWord Publishing, LLC
www.gracewordpublishing.com
U.S.A.

GRACEWORD PUBLISHING

Contents

To Theophilus – One Who Loves God

To make all men see what is the fellowship
of the mystery, which from the beginning
of the world hath been hid in God,
Who created all things by Jesus Christ

-Apostle Paul

Acknowledgements

I would like to thank those who were a source of support and encouragement. A special thanks to Steve and Stephanie Tackett who provided editorial advice. My unending gratitude to Frances Greene. A special thanks to T.B. Lang to whom some of the original letters to Theophilus were written.

Finally, I am grateful to you, the reader. What is a teacher without someone looking to learn? For those who want to learn more about the Bible, especially the end times, I thank God.

Foreword

GraceWord Publishing asked to write the forward to this book. I have known the author personally for several years. After he completed his second doctorate, he approached me to work with him on his post-doctoral work as he continued to test the system of theology explained in this book. Together we formed Grace Bible Network, a Bible educational group providing free online classes rightly dividing the Word of Truth. Classes are offered live and recorded. From the transcripts, he compiled and edited them into verse-by-verse biblical commentaries including Paul's epistles to the Romans and the Galatians.

I came to appreciate Dave's dedication and high energy. He has a heart for the Word of God. In this book he presents a summary of God's Word rightly divided. This will help anyone to understand the end times.

Rev. Steven L. Tackett

Preface

My background is neither a pastor nor am I affiliated with any sectarian group. I will not suggest you join any group, make any donation, or do anything. All I ask is that you sit back with an open mind. As you read the letters think about what is being presented even if it is not something you have heard before. We can understand other Christians better when we know what they believe. By doing so, we get a better understanding of other theological views.

In my previous profession, I was a property and casualty insurance agent. For insurance, everything centers around the insurance policy. I believe that is a key factor to my approach to the Bible.

Once someone buys an insurance policy (home, auto, boat) and has a claim, the policy coverage is determined by the coverage that was in effect at the time of the loss. Like a policy, the Bible says what it says whether we agree with it or not, or whether we read it or not. Our eternal destiny will be determined by what is written in the Bible. What we decide before we die will affect our future. For some reason, people fear what the Bible says. Is it too cumbersome to read? Do they feel it is outdated or no longer applicable? The foundation of faith for evangelical Christians is based upon the belief Scripture is inspired, infallible, complete, and authoritative. Take a look and you should find something to that effect included in your church's Statement of Faith published by most churches.

The Bible answers a lot of questions about God and man. It presents the pervasive problem of sin and God's singular solution. That is very good news indeed. No one should miss it because the good news is that it is free! For those who have difficulty with the Bible, there is a way to make understanding it a whole lot easier. It has to do with understanding the structure. Once someone understands the structure of the Bible, it not only becomes easier to understand, but is enjoyable too. The Bible is God's Word and, like God, His Word stands forever. After you understand it, it will never change. As an insurance agent, I found that the majority of policyholders never read their policy until it is too late. Sometimes, what they thought was covered is not, but then it is too late.

The Bible is the Word of God. Therefore, it is dependable – you can bet your life on it. This does not mean that people don't misinterpret it and, thereby, create what appears to be inconsistencies. Those would be the fruit of human carelessness. Remember it this way: God is on the hook with His book. The Bible is complete. The last verses in its final book, Revelation, make it clear that nothing can be added to or taken away from the text. Doing so will arouse the anger of God. Read the last four verses in the book of Revelation.

Additionally, the Bible is authoritative. This means there is no higher authority that supersedes the Word of God. It is God's direct revelation to mankind. It does not tell us *what we want to know*. It tells us *what God wants us to know*. It was written for that expressed singular purpose. There is one thing God cannot do. He cannot and will not change. Therefore, we can be confident that His Word will remain solid. For these reasons, we must rely upon His Word to provide us with answers to the end times.

You may be unfamiliar with my approach and it may be something new to you. If you think about it, that is actually good. If we read the same opinions and interpretations from the same people who agree with us on everything, then we will never learn more than what we already know. It will only appear to confirm what we already believe, whether it is true or not. So, if the end times seem uncertain, then perhaps you need to consider the Bible from a different approach. Each of us should be open-minded enough to allow the Bible to speak for itself.

In these letters, the Bible will be our only source and, since the Bible is the authority, biblical texts will be the center of our discussions. This may be something new to you, but it actually protects you from someone twisting the text to mean something else. It is typical in conversative biblical commentaries for that reason. I will be using the King James Version (KJV). Since I am comfortable with that text, I will provide you with assistance by adding comments within brackets. Textual references are included so that you can easily find and read the texts within their biblical context for yourself. In fact, I would encourage you to always read verses within their context.

When you read the letters, consider an attorney presenting his argument before a judge and jury. You can be either, but you would be obligated to listen to a presentation of facts concerning the case. So too, the judge must assure that it is done without prejudice. The evidence must be weighed carefully before coming to a verdict. It will be the attorney's job to present the detailed information in the most concise and understandable way he or she can. However, the decision is up to each juror.

I usually like to begin a class by asking two questions. Let me ask you the first: *How much do you trust Jesus on a scale of 1 to 10?* Now, you need to remember that number. The second is: *On the same scale of 1 to 10, how much do you trust the Bible?* They usually wonder how do these two questions relate. It is simple. The Bible is called both *the Word of God* and *the Living Word* for a reason. In the Gospel of John, the apostle writes at the very beginning in verse 1:1:

> 1 **In the beginning was <u>the Word</u>, and <u>the Word</u> was with God, and <u>the Word</u> was God.**

John makes it even clearer in verse 14:

> 14 **And <u>the Word</u> was made flesh, and dwelt among us . . .**

So, *the Word* is equal to God. He became *flesh* or *human*. Therefore, if you say you trust Jesus, and I sincerely hope you do, then the measure of your trust for Jesus is how much you trust the *Word of God.* How did your two answers compare and why is this so important? God used men to write down His revelation. It was done through the inspiration of the Holy Spirit (i.e., divine), but it was written by the hands of men (i.e., human). We need to stop and think about this. John tells us that God was the Word (i.e., divine) and that He became flesh (i.e., human) and dwelt among us. If we think about it, then this means the Bible is both human and divine as well. Now, can you think of any person who is both human and divine? There is only one answer and that answer is Jesus Christ. The Bible is equal to God. They both have the authority of God. This should establish the importance of the Bible.

Here is an interesting point. When Jesus returns at HIs Second Coming, He is riding a white horse. We are told His name. Do you know what it is? Read in Revelation 19:11-13:

> 11 **And I saw heaven opened, and behold a white horse; and he that sat upon him was called Faithful and True, and in righteousness he doth judge and make war. 12 His eyes were as a flame of fire, and on his head were many crowns; and he had a name written, that no man knew, but he himself.**

13 And he was clothed with a vesture dipped in blood: and his name is called <u>The Word of God.</u>

Most people miss this. So, you might want to read that last verse again. The very same Jesus who many Christians claim to adore, when He returns at the Second Coming, look at His name! His name is *The Word of God!*

Instead of wanting to know Jesus Christ as *The Word of God*, they would rather experience Him through worship. That all sounds good until you realize the difference. Reading the Bible, God is speaking to you. Worshipping Him, you are speaking words of praise to Him. There is certainly nothing wrong with worship and the worship experience. However, any true relationship can only be based upon a relationship with *The Word of God*. That is the only way. It is work and will take time, but it is our testimony of our love of Him Who saved us. Someone may ask, "Rather than read the Bible myself, why can't someone just tell me what to believe?" Surely, they can! In fact, that is exactly what many are doing today and it is well worth their time financially!

Let us consider the Pharisees and what Jesus said to them by quoting Isaiah in Mark 7:7-9:

7 Howbeit in vain [self-centeredness] do they worship me, <u>teaching for doctrines the commandments [or traditions] of men</u>.

8 For <u>laying aside [the Word of God] the commandment of God</u>, [instead] ye hold <u>the tradition of men</u> . . .

9 And he said unto them, Full well ye reject the [Word of God] commandment of God, that ye may keep [the traditions of men which is] your own tradition.

As such, we must honor God's Word and avoid the traditions of man. We must ask God to open our minds to understanding His Word. The Holy Spirit inspired the writers and He will also reveal its truth to those who ask.

This style of this book is as a compilation of letters addressed to Theophilus. *Theophilus* means *one who loves God.* I am writing these letters to someone who is already a Christian and wants a deeper understanding of God. It was the Apostle Luke who wrote both the Gospel of Luke and the Acts of the Apostles. In each, he addressed them to *Theophilus* because, he too, was writing to *one who loves God.*

This book will provide you with the means by which you can understand the Bible as a whole. If you are interested in the end times, then it will provide you with the tools necessary for you to accomplish that.

Those who truly seek to know God through His Son, the Word of God, will be blessed.

Introduction

To Theophilus:

Our goal is to have you understand the end times and there is only one way to do this. We must get you to where you can understand the Bible as a whole, not necessarily all the details, but at least its overall structure. The easiest way to do this is start with an outline to simplify its structure. Creating a framework will provide us with solid ground; a foundation upon which we can build your understanding. Without a framework, everything that we learn about God is filed in our memory under a heading of *my thoughts about God*. There is a word that means exactly that – *the study or knowledge of God*. The word is *theology*.

Many people have told me, emphatically, they *do not studied theology*. They are confusing theology with religion. I do suggest they studied *theology* academically. We all collect bits and pieces of biblical facts as well as our own views and opinions about

God – whether they are true or not. Knowledge of the existence of God is part of our inherent conscience – our God-given knowledge of the existence of God. Everyone has a theology – even the atheist. The theological belief of the atheist is simple: there is no God. Everything that we read or listen to that tells us, or alleges to tell us, about God gives us either information or opinions, true or false, about Him. What we choose to retain in our memory is our individual choice. Therefore, what we choose to believe about God is our *theology*.

Now, let us look at the way we organize our *theology*. As rational beings, we create a structure or filing system in our minds. It is our way to organize these thoughts and memories. Later, this helps us to recall those memories. This ordering of our thoughts will remain unchanged unless something challenges it. Until then, everything remains status quo – as is.

This is exactly what happened to me while I was attending seminary. Later on, I will share the details with you. For now, here is an example. Let us say that you were told and subsequently chose to believe that A equals B. Later, you were taught and believed that B equals C. These facts are securely held in your memory. However, much later, you come to find out that A does not equal C. This would be an example of a conflict. When I teach, I use this example. Conflict can be a good thing because with conflict comes resolution. I am referring here to rational thinking. The way we mentally organize our beliefs is done by creating a *system* of interrelated thoughts about a subject. In this case, it would be a *theological system.*

Our rational thinking organizes our thoughts like a library's catalog or index of books. If our *system* fails or is proven to be false, then it creates a *crisis.* Our minds typically work, whether subconsciously or consciously, to seek a logical solution until the crisis is resolved. Alternatively, some may choose to ignore the conflict by rationalizing it away. They may be willing to hold the conflict "in tension" only to deal with it later. Having your beliefs challenged is a growing experience. We should be challenged. It will strengthen our existing *system* by confirming what we know or it will cause us to consider other perspectives. That choice remains ours to make.

Before we can understand the end times, we need to think about what we believe and why we believe it. The *Word of God* alone must be the basis of our beliefs. Throughout these letters, we will include what is referred to as *proof texts.* There is a reason why the biblical texts are provided. It is important for us to verify for ourselves what is being discussed is in total agreement with *The Word of God*. It is very difficult for someone to twist the Word of God when they are printed on the page in front of them. If we seek *truth*, then we must confine ourselves to the biblical text.

Let us consider the concept of *truth*. It will play an important role in our ability to test to see if something is true or not. Finding biblical truths is our goal. There are two types: *absolute* truth and *relative* truth. What is the difference? *Absolute truth* does not change. It remains constant and applies universally; not to just one or more persons. However, *relative truth* applies individually and may not necessarily apply to anyone else. For example, the statement from one person that "liver is delicious" may be true for one, but not true for everyone else. Therefore, *relative truth* is subjective or individual by its nature.

Absolute truth, which is the truth we seek, is never determined by popularity. A question I pose to my students is this: How many people does it take to make something true? After some discussion and thought, they conclude that truth is not dependent upon how many people believe it or agree upon it. *Truth stands alone!*

It is important that we remember the Bible is *absolute truth* because it is God's truth. It does not change. It remains constant and it applies universally. The *Word of God* is His revelation to His Creatures. God intended that this message have a singular meaning. It is not to be interpreted by individual whim or fancy. This is important because we will be discussing a "test of truth" in a moment. The truth we are looking to find cannot be inconsistent. It cannot have conflicts with its interpretation. It cannot change over the course of time nor in different situations. Jesus Christ is the *Word of God.* He is the same yesterday, today, and tomorrow. If this is true, and I believe that it is, then the singular interpretation of biblical text can and must be tested! How can we test our interpretation of truth?

We must consider the Bible in its entirety. Like an insurance policy the Bible is one singular document even though it is comprised of many sections or books. Since the Bible is *absolute truth,* written by God, conflict cannot exist within the document. That would be inconceivable in a document created by God. We must trust His Word as the absolute authority. Therefore, we will not question His Word, but apply a *test of truth* to its interpretation. As we consider building a *system of theology* it must (1) apply to the entire Bible from beginning to end and (2) there can be no conflicts within its application. If there are, then it will be back to the drawing board again.

Within existing evangelical or Bible-preaching churches, there are three prevalent *systems of theology* being used. In seminary, I was required to study all three *systems* at great length and understand each of them. Most Christians are unaware there is more than one *system of theology* since they have only been taught one. If this applies to you, then this book will be a real eye-opener. Do not feel bad as most Christians believe whatever they are being taught is the only "correct" interpretation. The thought of challenging some teachers or preachers would be anathema. Every Bible teacher or preacher is using one or more of these three systems. On the other hand, some Christians over a period of time attend a lot of different churches. Since they learn under various pastors, there is no wonder they feel confused as if the Bible contradicts itself. I assure you that is not the case. They have what I call a "blenderized" *system of theology*. This will make understanding the Bible very difficult for them.

Since each of us who has been taught is affected by one of more of these three *systems of theology*, it is important that we take time to identify them. They are as follows: existential, covenant, and dispensational. All of these three *systems* uses the same Bible!

Most seminaries produce graduates who carry on their approved customs, traditions, and philosophies of men. This is especially true if the school is dedicated to a particular denomination that promotes a particular *system*. In seminary, I was required to study all three systems in depth. Each of these *systems* sees the same Bible differently. Therefore, each yields a different result. Now, you can understand why there are so many different churches out there. What initially made these differences was their indivudual *system of theology*.

I understand that what I am writing may offend some people. No one wants to be told they may be wrong. It is certainly not my intention to alienate anyone. You alone are the one who decides what you will and will not believe. Think about this point. We know what we know because that was what we were taught to know. Education seems to be a process of teaching someone something and then measuring or testing them to see if they learned what they were taught. However, what is being taught as truth is rarely questioned. It is just assumed to be true and believed to be true.

Anything we learn subsequent to establishing our *system of theology* is then viewed from within that existing system. This book will allow you to think about your existing *system* as it presents you with alternatives. Changing or updating your system, whatever you accept to be true, will be completely up to you. Frequently, people will seek out those who also believe what they believe. They do this to reassure them that what they believe is true. Finding out differently, upsets the apple cart. No one wants to find out that what they believe is wrong. There is a better way and you can do it yourself. We do this by testing our *system of theology* sooner rather than later.

Consider this example. To following is an example of certain people are having their *system of theology* challenged. You can imagine their consternation. We read about them in the gospels. The Pharisees could be described as the best and well educated of those in Judaism at the time. They were taught certain views of Scripture and then perpetuated those same beliefs for generations. Speaking to the Pharisees, Jesus said in Mark 7:7-8:

> 7 **Howbeit in vain do they [the people] worship me, [for you are] <u>teaching for doctrines the commandments of men</u>.**

8 For <u>laying aside [ignoring] the commandment of God, [and instead] ye [teach them to] hold the tradition of men . . .</u>

We must let the Bible speak for itself. It is Christ, the *Word of God,* Who is speaking. You can read the verses above either with or without the comments. The comments were added to help understand the point that Jesus was making. The word *doctrine* means *teaching.* Here, Jesus is referring to the teachings from God's Word. Since space is limited, please be sure to read any original text within its context. We should do that for all Bible teaching.

The Bible is God's revelation to man. It is His message to him. If evil is considered to be *lies and deception*, then Satan wars against God and His believers by attacking the *Word of God!* Jesus called Satan the father of *lies.* Those who are liars He called the children of their father, the Devil. Do you remember Jesus' testing in the wilderness? Every time Satan tested Jesus, what did Jesus do? He responded with "It is written . . ." and quoted Scripture to rebuke Satan who was twisting God's Word. Satan created false versions of the Bible by grossly misinterpreting God's truth in order to confuse people. I cannot stress this enough. The Bible stands alone in its authority and power to change people's lives. Here is what the writer of Hebrews wrote in verse 4:12:

> 12 For <u>the word of God</u> is quick, and powerful, and sharper than any two-edged sword, piercing even to the dividing asunder of soul and spirit, and of the joints and marrow, and is a discerner of the thoughts and intents of the heart.

Here is one final thought. Let us consider the role the Holy Spirit plays in our understanding of the Bible. It is the Holy Spirit Who *illuminates* or opens our eyes to understand the *Word of God*. I speak from experience. The Holy Spirit will give you understanding if you ask for it and are willing to wait for His response. The asking is easy. The waiting is hard. Therefore, as you read this book, ask the Holy Spirit if what I am telling you is true. Ask His to confirm it for you. Then, keep your eyes open, have faith, and He will give you the answer.

Your brother in Christ,
Dr. David Alan Greene

Chapter 1

To Theophilus:

I am excited to begin. We will be using what I call the *test of truth* as we move forward. We will continually apply this test to interpretations. It has only two rules. First, the same *system of theology* or system by which we interpret the Bible must be applied to the whole Bible. In other words, it must be comprehensively applied to the Bible from beginning to end. There can be no switching horses in the middle of the race. Second, when applying a particular *system of theology* to any portion of Scripture, it cannot contradict any other portion of the Scripture. If it does, then its failure will automatically invalidate that system. We have certainly set a high standard to meet, as well we should. This is the *Word of God*.

Earlier, I mentioned that I personally had a "theological crisis." Let me share my story with you. During my studies for the Master of Biblical Studies, I learned that "with crisis comes resolution." It was actually a blessing because, at that point, the Holy Spirit became my teacher. This only applies to those who are interested in seeking resolution since many people do not care. It happened while I was living in rural New Hampshire where I was attending my daughter's baptism at a local Baptist Church. Their interim pastor was a retired pastor with his doctorate. I looked forward to hearing what he had to say. During his sermon, he referred to verses from Ephesians. He said, "We all know that we are saved by grace though faith without works" to which there was a resounding "Amen." Then, he continued, "But . . ." and paused for dramatic effect before he continued, ". . .we all know that without good works we can lose our salvation." That statement was the cause of my theological conflict! Why? It was because it failed the second test of truth. Did I hear him correctly? No one else seemed to be bothered by this or had even noticed. So, let me get this straight. He said we were saved by God's gift and not by works, however, if we wanted to keep the gift, then we had to work for it. Does that seem like a contradiction to you? It did to me.

If something causes a conflict with what we currently believe, then I believe it will be for the best. We all need to trust in the Holy Spirit we read the Bible. All I ask is that you prayerfully consider what is being presented here. I have no ax to grind. I do not belong to any group that I will ask you to join. I will fellowship with any who believe in the death, burial, and resurrection of our Lord and Savior Jesus Christ. These letters are written to them.

If you are reading this letter, then I trust you have a heart for God. These letters are addressed "To Theophilus" which means "To One Who Loves God." It is for that reason that I am investing my time in writing these letters to you. We will delve deep into the Scriptures and I assure you that your investment in time will be well worth it. The finished work of Christ is sufficient for our salvation. Many will agree with that statement. It is what is added to this statement that diminishes its effective value.

The Bible is authoritative, complete, and without error. It is God-breathed as its writers were *inspired by the Holy Spirit*. As humans, we are subject to error because of the Fall. The method by which we choose to read and understand the truth is important. We must seek the guidance of the Holy Spirit. Our understanding must be *illuminated by the Holy Spirit*. Consider the Pharisees. They were highly educated men with the equivalence of a doctorate in law. They too were earnestly committed to studying Scripture and could recite endless verses from memory. They knew the Scriptures. Yet, Jesus had a very low opinion of their understanding. So, if these learned men veered off into the pucker brush, what is to say that highly educated people of today are not doing the same thing?

We can have a general knowledge of the existence of God from observing His creation. That is referred to as *general revelation*. However, any specific knowledge God wants us to know must come from Him. He must reveal it to us. This is *special revelation*. The Bible is exactly that. It is God's revelation of Himself and His plan to those interested. Therefore, if it is God's intent to reveal His truth, then He would certainly intend that man be able to understand it. God spoke to Abraham. Abraham understood what God said and he believed it. Otherwise, God would not have counted Abraham's faith as righteousness. (See Gen. 15:6.) We too are in the same situation today. God is speaking to us through the *Word of God*. Let us not forget Who is speaking. It is His desire for us to understand it and believe it. If we are to believe God, then we must be able to do so. 1 Timothy 2:3-4:

> **3 For this is good and acceptable in the sight of God our Saviour; 4 Who will have all men to be saved, and to come unto the knowledge of the truth.**

4

God desires for each of us to come to the saving knowledge of His truth! That is the purpose of this book. What you do with that knowledge is based upon your own individual free will to choose.

It is important to put human commentary in perspective. Commentary, good or bad, is nothing more than learned theologians interpreting the Bible. Each is applying their own chosen *system of theology*. This applies to me as well. Commentary should never be elevated a status of being equal in authority to Scripture. Here is another story.

I was teaching a Men's Bible study. We all had our Bibles open. I had just finished reading the text from the Bible. Suddenly, the person sitting next to me said, "That's not what my Bible says!" Being still new to this, I decided not to panic but instead ask a question. "Frank, what version of the Bible are you using?" He was using the NIV. I thought that should be fine. So, I asked him to show me where he was reading. It turned out to be the new NIV Study Bible and he was reading from the commentary below the text. Since it was "in the Bible," it must be true, right? They all looked at me like I was selling a used car that was a lemon. I explained that commentary is someone's opinion. The point was made that since it was in the Bible it must be someone who knows the truth, right? I asked, "You're saying this guy must have at least his doctorate, right?" They agreed. To which I replied, "Look, I have my doctorate and I am telling you I disagree with this fellow's commentary." I went on to explain exactly why. The man beside me was a dear brother in Christ. He had been an evangelical Christian for over thirty years and attended conservative Bible-preaching churches. My point is that commentary is never equal to Scripture regardless of who it is.

I had a discussion with a former insurance client about salvation. He told me he was all set and didn't need to hear what I had to say. He told me he had spent a whole day with his episcopalian priest and they had talked about salvation. He told me this priest was really a great guy. The priest had assured him that he had nothing to worry about. So, he was willing to bet his salvation not on the *Word of God*, but on the word of a priest who was using his own system of interpretation. He made it clear he did not want to hear anything about the Bible from me. Eventually, he will find out if he is right.

A child might look at all the different Christian churches and say there are a ga-zillion of them. Each one offering something different. Most churches try to meet the social and emotional needs of attendees. Let us limit our discussion to evangelical churches alone. These would be the churches with an apparent high view of Scripture. Some Christians scoff at Scripture thinking that it is no longer relevant. Do they realize Who they are dismissing? They claim to love Jesus, but dismiss the *Word of God* from the Church? Jesus is the *Word of God!*

Some Christians believe God is still speaking today through modern-day prophets. They give the Church prophecies and words of wisdom as God's representatives. The office of prophet is outlined in the Old Testament. Prophets must be authenticated by miracles, signs, and wonders by God to be validated as His spokesperson. Prophets were God's instruments through whom He would speak to Israel. Those who claimed to be prophets and were not, were to be stoned to death as punishment. At the end of the Bible, God makes an important point. Revelation 22: 18-19:

> 18 **For I testify unto every man that heareth the words of the prophecy of this book, <u>If any man shall add unto these things,</u> God shall add unto him the plagues that are written in this book:**

19 And <u>if any man shall take away from the words of the book of this prophecy,</u> God shall take away his part out of the book of life, and out of the holy city, and from the things which are written in this book.

Certain actions concerning God's Word have consequences. I do not believe that He is limiting these warnings to the book of Revelation alone. Do we really need more than what God has already given us? Can there be anything more than the *Word of God* Himself? The answer is found in 2 Timothy 4:3-4

3 For the time will come when they will not endure sound doctrine; but after their own lusts shall they heap to themselves teachers, having itching ears;

4 And they shall turn away their ears from the truth, and shall be turned unto fables.

There are three predominant *systems of theology*. Each has its own means and method of interpretation. In the next letter, we will begin to examine each of these *systems of interpretation* one at a time and provide examples. In the meantime, consider this. Every Bible teacher or preacher uses, either knowingly or unknowingly, one or more of these systems. From that system, they study, interpret, and teach the Bible to others. Soon, you will be able to listen to someone teach or preach and be able to identify which system they are using.

As always, I look forward to our next letter.

In Christ,
Dr. David Alan Greene

Chapter 2

To Theophilus:

Each of my letters will build upon the previous. It is my hope that you can sense my passion for teaching someone how to understand God's Word. I give it great thought as to how best to present the information to you in a clear and concise manner. Remember, our free will determines whether we choose to agree or not. We have our free will which is our freedom to choose for ourselves what we will and will not accept. So, enjoy thinking about the options!

Here is a bold statement. No one ever wants to be told they are wrong, especially the longer they have believed something to be true. New students have fresh minds and are eager to learn. As we get older, it is natural to be more confident that what we believe is the truth. Concerning the Bible, it is almost impossible for us to change our minds without the direct intervention of the Holy Spirit. It was certainly a challenge for me. I began my Master's degree at age 55. I was already a grandpa!

At some point, we pass the stage of investigative research having an open and inquiring mind. Perhaps we still need to consider the possibility there are other choices of which we were unaware. People can only make their decisions based upon information available to them at the time. In other words, our choices may have been made from limited information. Here, I am speaking specifically about the Bible. Here is a question for you. What would you do if another valid alternative, previously unknown, was presented? Would you at least consider it?

As Christians, our theological beliefs becomes the lens through which we have our world view. Some call it a *philosophy of life*. An atheist has a system of theology believing that there is no god. They see everything through that world view. I believe that no one can truly understand the Bible without applying a valid *system of theology* to its interpretation. I have watched people try to do it. Determined to read the Bible in a year, they read it from Genesis to Revelation like it was a novel. When they are done, they know what it says, but are only confused. They may talk to friends, family, and their pastor all of whom apply a different *systems of theology*.

I mentioned there are three predominant *systems*. People who are truly interested in understanding the Bible should be aware of all three. Not only will they understand the options, but they will also be able to identify someone else's approach to the Bible. During Jesus' earthly ministry, He presented a different interpretation of Scripture from what the ruling Pharisees taught. As the Jews listened, they had free will to choose who they would believe. They could believe the Son of God or they could choose to hold firmly to the traditions, customs, and philosophies of men. It was their choice.

By the end of this book, you will be able to choose which system of theology you want to use. Most Christians never have this opportunity. They go to church, whatever brand or flavor they chose, and listen to the preacher present his or her sermon. These preachers are the teachers of their congregations. First, most of them are using only one of the three *systems.* Second, most sermons or lessons today are *topical.* A preacher picks a particular topic from Scripture. Then, they find various verses from anywhere in the Bible to support their conclusion. Yes, the verses are taken from the Bible but, generally, are read out of context. Most sermons are designed to elicit emotional responses or motivate the hearers *to do* something. Yet, all of them will emphatically state that they "preach from the Bible." However, do they "teach from the Bible" or present their own opinions? Theophilus, you should know that there is a huge difference!

In many contemporary churches, I have found that the driving force in their services is the band. There is nothing wrong with worship as long as the *Word of God* is the center. Music as a medium is designed to create an *emotional response* based upon their experience. However, the Bible is designed to create a *rational response*. Imagine an emotion-driven church inviting Jesus Christ to personally speak at their church. He walks to the pulpit, stands there, and slowly scans the faces of the attendees. Do you think they would listen to Him speak to them? If the answer is "yes," then perhaps the pastor should preach from the Bible and allow the *Word of God* to speak to them. Unfortunately, I believe that most would prefer to be entertained. Many came to see Jesus because they wanted to experience His miracles. They did not come to listen to Him teach, but to be entertained. Going home, they left no different than they had come – empty souls without salvation. Please remember this concept of an emotion-driven seeker as it will become relevant later.

Many evangelical churches have weekly Bible Studies. Ask them what book they are studying and they will give the name of a contemporary popular Christian author. He or she giving their own view and application of Scripture. Today, there is very little teaching of Scripture itself. I consider that to be teaching the Bible verse-by-verse. This is a different style than *topical* teaching. It is known as *expository* teaching because it teaches what the Bible says. Expository teaching has the highest view of Scripture. We will be using *expository* teaching in this book. This method of teaching uses literal-historical-grammatical interpretation. They study and ask questions like this: What is the message? From whom was this message given and for whom was it intended? Those who answer those questions get closer to the true meaning of Scripture. Once some simple tools are learned, it is very easy. The golden nuggets you find in God's truth makes it all worthwhile.

We are laying the groundwork here. We need to use only one *system* and that *system* must pass *the test of truth*. That test will be: (1) one singular *system of interpretation* must be applied to the entire *Word of God* and (2) it must not fail by contradicting or conflicting with any other portion of Scripture. God's Word is perfect and any apparent contradictions in His Word are, therefore, man-made.

We may be different interpretations, but there is only one question we must ask, "What does the Bible say?" Knowing the predominant *systems of theology* and their differences will help you to understand the confusion in Christianity today. We will limit ourselves to only *evangelical* churches who preach from the Bible. I separated them into three groups: existential, covenantal, and dispensational. We will delve into each and provide you with a summary. If you attend an evangelical church, you may be able to see your assembly in one or more of these.

We will start with *Existential Theology*. Existentialism is based on perceived experiences – past, present, and future. So too is superstition. An event happening must be a sign from God directed specifically at you. Falling on ice on the stairs while going to church does not mean that God didn't want you to go. It simply means someone should have sanded the stairs because they were icy. Revelation from God seems to come to individuals who are then left trying to interpret their experiences as a message from a higher power. These people tend to gather together with those who have similar "experiences." When it comes to the Bible, they interpret verses based upon their own personal experiences. I have another story to give you an example.

I had been teaching a men's Bible class at a Baptist church for some time. I was standing in line at the covered-dish dinner following the Sunday service. An older man in his mid-eighties was attending my class. He said, "I've never been to a Bible study like yours before and I've gone to this church my whole life." Rather than respond, I probed for more information, "What were the other Bible studies like?" He said, "Someone would read a verse and then we'd go around the table and each person would say what that particular verse meant to them." That is an example of existential interpretation. Existentialism is not concerned with *who* is talking, *to whom* it is talking, *when* the message was given, or *what* the message was. Nope! It is all about what it means to each of them individually.

Many Charismatic and Pentecostal churches are driven by personal experiences. The value of the *Word of God* is diminished while current prophecies and words of knowledge make people stand in awe of these modern-day prophets. Are they demonstrating the gifts of the Spirit? Therefore, the *Word of God* is no longer speaking. When the Bible is used, it is often used out of context to support their own individual views.

Therefore, *Existential Theology* is actually a means of using of the Bible and not an interpretation. This is not a *system of interpretation*. It is subjective which means the interpretation of the Bible is centered around a person's emotions and experience. Therefore, their conclusions can only be *relative* truth and not the *absolute* truth for which we are searching. An example of *relative* truth would be someone saying that liver is delicious. Their system is consistently inconsistent and, therefore, for our purpose, it cannot qualify as a valid *system* of interpretation.

I had a conversation with someone who was involved in a church that taught that God could not be "contained" in a book. They encouraged God to speak through their individual members. Think about that for a moment. Earlier I spoke about divinity and humanity being combined into One. We saw that Jesus Christ is both fully man (human) and fully God (divine). The Bible was inspired by God (divine) and written by men (human) who were inspired by the Holy Spirit. We are told about the *Word of God* being in the beginning. John 1:1:

> 1 **In the beginning was the Word, and the Word was with God, and the Word was God.**

At the conclusion of the Bible, the same apostle tell us about the Rider on the white horse Whose name was Faithful and True. Revelation 19:13:

13 **And he was clothed with a vesture dipped in blood: and his name is called The Word of God.**

Jesus Christ is the beginning and the end. He is the *Word of God!*

You may be able to recognize existential churches from these characteristics. By removing or diminishing the authority of the Bible, they can bestow that authority upon other individuals. They can either interpret the Bible according to their own individual experiences or they can proclaim themselves to be prophets and speak on behalf of God. You might see a banner hanging on front of their church building saying, "God is still speaking!" They believe that God is currently speaking to them through their experiences, their emotions, and modern-day prophets. Whether it is intuition or superstition, it is not a singular, comprehensive *system* of interpretation.

Furthermore, for this group, it does not matter whether it contradicts other portions of Scripture or not. They have the individual freedom to add, change, and remove offensive Scripture. This would mean that, as a *system of interpretation*, it would fail the second test of truth as well. So, here is some good news. There are only two more *systems of theology* to examine. Please allow me to ask you a question. Do you think that, now, sitting in an unfamiliar church that you could determine if they were *existentialists?*

We will continue with the second *system of interpretation* in the next letter.

In His service,
Dr. David Alan Greene

Chapter 3

To Theophilus:

Now, we will move on to *Covenant Theology*. We know that God makes covenants with whomever He chooses. Most Christians are familiar with the concept of the "covenant of marriage." Since this is a covenant instituted by God, traditional Jewish husbands and wives sign a marriage contract when they are married. What is it that makes *covenants* different from other legal agreements? God is a party to a *covenant*. Regardless of the number people involved, if God is included, then it is a *covenant*. Therefore, it is considered to be eternally binding, unalterable, and unbreakable. Let us look at some of the *covenants* that God made in the Old Testament.

It is important for me to interject some information for those who might not be familiar with how Israel got its name. Abraham gave birth to his son named Isaac. Isaac gave birth to Jacob. Jacob wrestled with God and God changed his name to Israel. So, Jacob and Israel are the same person. That is how Abraham's descendants became known as *the children of Israel.*

What *covenant theology* teaches, having studied many of their most prominent theologians, is that God made covenants with Israel. Most Christians would agree with that. However, they believe that these covenants which God made with Israel, collectively. They also believe that these covenants were later transferred to the "Church" who are "the true people of God." The Jews rejected their Messiah or the Christ. At that point, the "Church" *replaced* Israel when it comes to the covenants and promises God made. How is this possible? Briefly, here is a quick summary of their rationale. God chose the Jews. They were God's chosen people. The Jews rejected their Messiah and had Him crucified. The "Church" was those believers who followed after the crucifixion. They replaced Israel as God's "chosen people." Therefore, the promises and covenants which God made with Israel now belong to the "Church."

Some denominations are known forteaching *Covenant Theology.* These would include Presbyterians, Anglicans, Lutherans, and Catholics. Each of these uses *Covenant Theology* as their *system of interpretation*. At another covered dish supper, I was sitting with the visiting pastor who was a Presbyterian. I asked him a question: "Do you believe in the covenant of marriage?" After being highly offended that I should ask him such a foolish question, he responded that he did. I then asked, "Can you transfer a marriage covenant from one wife to another?" A look of horror came over his face. He was appalled! I assured him it was a hypothetical question. "Absolutely not!" He explained that once a covenant was made it could not be broken. He assured me that an existing covenant could not be transferred to someone else. It would be impossible. I found his answer interesting considering that *Covenant Theology* is called "replacement theology" for this very reason.

When I was in my early seminary years, one of my textbooks used the words "the church in the wilderness." What? I thought the church started in Acts 2! Having never heard that before, I called my professor to ask him about it. He told me the book must have been written by a covenant theologian since they see the "Church" as being "God's people" regardless of the time period. So, they believe that God's people, regardless of who they are or what point in time, are the "Church." This may stem from the origins of the word "church."

If we look at the origin of the word *church*, we find that it comes from the Greek word *ekklesia* meaning *the called-out ones*. Logically, could say that the *ekklesia* is a subset from a larger set of people. That is true. However, the word *ekklesia* used in Acts 19:23-41 is translated as *assembly*. Paul used the word the same word *ekklesia* to denote an angry mob in Ephesus. This mob was furious over the damage Paul had caused to their silver idols' trade. So, the angry mob who were a smaller portion, or subset, of all the citizens in Ephesus was called an *ekklesia* by Paul. This angry mob protesting against Paul's ministry were certainly not the "church."

In covenant theology, it is their fixed belief that the "Church" is one singular group of people called-out by God. This is something unique to *Covenant Theology*. God chose Abraham, Isaac, and Jacob. They were *the called-out ones* whom God chose. They were His "chosen people." To this, I would whole-heartedly agree. The problem is when their concept expands to include all of the people whom God has *called out*. They believe there can be only one singular group and that group is the "Church."

We know that the covenants made by God are permanent. They are irrevocable, unalterable, and they are non-transferrable. God does not change and neither does His Word. He neither retracts His Word nor changes His mind. When the Jews denied their Messiah and had Him put to death, the covenant theologians believe that the disciples, His true followers, continued on as the "Church." According to *Covenant Theology*, it is this new group of believers, now mostly Gentiles, to whom these promises and covenants belong.

If Jesus' earthly ministry included Gentiles, then consider the following. All of His twelve apostles were Jewish and not Gentiles. What if we found conclusive evidence that Christ's earthly ministry was exclusively to the Jews and not to the Gentiles? Always look at the biblical evidence. The Lord Jesus Himself gives instructions to the Twelve in Matthew 10:5-6:

> 5 **These twelve Jesus sent forth, and commanded them, saying, <u>Go not into the way of the Gentiles, [nor] and into any city of the Samaritans enter ye not:</u> 6 But [instead] <u>go rather to the lost sheep of the house of Israel</u>.**

Wait! To whom are the Twelve to go? It looks like they were to go *exclusively* to Israel – *the lost sheep of the house of Israel*. In other words, their message was to be delivered to the Jews. This will make sense later as we move through the Bible.

Let us not forget. One of the *tests of truth* was *failure.* Only one failure is needed to disqualify a system, but there are other conflicts too. The Apostle Paul made a statement to the Gentiles in Rome concerning Christ's earthly ministry. Paul is known as the Apostle to the Gentiles (*cf.* Rom. 11:13, 1 Tim. 2:7; 2 Tim. 1:11). In writing to the Gentile believers, Paul said something very interesting. Romans 15:8:

> 8 **Now I say that Jesus Christ was <u>a minister of the circumcision</u> for the truth of God, <u>to confirm the promises made unto the fathers:</u>**

In the Abrahamic Covenant, God required that all Jewish males be circumcised as a physical mark of the covenant. Because of this requirement, the Jews are often referred to collectively as *the Circumcision.* According to Paul, Jesus Christ came "to confirm the promises made unto the fathers." Here, the word "confirm" means "to affirm, fulfill, or validate" the promises. Who are *the fathers?* They are the ones to whom the promises were made: Abraham, Isaac, and Jacob!

Jesus did not go to the Gentiles, but instead went to the lost sheep of Israel. Covenant theologians

26

are right about Israel. However, by rationalizing, they have reasoned that Israel is no longer the "called-out ones" and, therefore, no longer the recipients of God's covenants and promises. We have more evidence to the contrary.

Most seminary students are required to study church history. Briefly, following the Apostolic Age, it morphed into the Patristic Age who were the early "church fathers." This was not God's doing, but that of humans! Man worked to consolidate all the believers into one Church and, under its control, it usurped God's authority. The *Word of God* lost His authority. To manage and control believers, a hierarchy of leadership was established. Their purpose was to rule and supervise the followers. Augustine was a dynamic force in the creation of the Holy Catholic Church. Here, the word "catholic" means "universal."

The Reformers separated from the "Holy Catholic Church" to return to their biblical roots. However, now detached from the Pope and the rule of Rome, many of their core beliefs remained the same. Much of Covenant Theology came from Augustine where the Old Testament is for the *Jews* while the New Testament is for the "Church." Let us look at an Old Testament prophecy concerning the New Covenant. Many Christians are taught that Christ made this new covenant with His Gentile Church. However, let us look at the prophet Jeremiah who foretold of this New Covenant. Let us see exactly with whom God will make this New Covenant.

Taking quotes out of context can be dangerous because it leads to the possibility of misinterpretation. We need to begin at a point where it identifies to whom God is speaking. Jeremiah 31:31-32:

> **31 Behold, the days come, saith the LORD, that I will make a <u>new covenant</u> with <u>the house of Israel</u>, <u>and</u> with <u>the house of Judah</u>:**

> **32 Not according to the covenant that I made <u>with their fathers</u> in the day that I took them by the hand <u>to bring them out of the land of Egypt</u>; which my covenant they brake, although I was an husband unto them, saith the LORD:**

The above verses make it pretty clear. God said He will make this new covenant with Israel and Judah. He confirms this by referring to the former covenant He made "with their fathers." That would be the Mosaic Covenant where God took them by the hand and led them out of Egypt. Can there be any question to

28

whom God was speaking? These are the same people as "the lost sheep of the house of Israel" (Matt. 10:6). Jesus Christ came to confirm the promises "made to their fathers" (Jer. 31:32). They are Abraham, Isaac, and Jacob and their children.

Covenants are not transferable. They cannot be broken. If we believe that the promises God made to the Jews will not come true, then we question the veracity of Scripture and the integrity of God. The old covenant does not go away. Think about this. What if the requirements of the old covenant God made with Israel are to be fulfilled by God through His Son? Then, the old covenant would remain in full force and effect. One of the parties fulfilled the obligations of both parties! I am sitting here thinking about this. There is no other word I can use but Wow!

Covenant Theology has a massive number of adherents. To challenge their belief system and its associated traditions would require someone bold with a brave heart just like the Apostle Paul. I am sure there are people who will read this in total disagreement. Disagree with me if you choose, but each of us is subject to the test of truth regardless of who we are and what we choose to believe.

Our purpose here is not to argue theology, but to understand the Bible in general and the end times specifically. Let us agree to hold this matter in tension for a moment. *Covenant Theology* will be better understood when we compare side-by-side with the third and final *system of interpretation*. Both *systems* hold a high view of Scripture. Where they differ is in the application of their *system of interpretation*. The results produce drastically different conclusions concerning the end times. So, we must press on toward our goal of understanding the Scripture in general and the end times specifically.

If a system failure occurs, the problem should not be rationalized away by making excuses or defending the failure. A man who is defending his systems could say, "Certainly, my system is not flawed. I will continue to believe it and allow it to 'live in tension' until the Lord is able to explain it to me." That is allegiance to a particular *system* or *tradition*. It is not allegiance to the *Word of God*. The Bible is God's means of sending a message to man. Therefore, that message, contained in the Bible, must be flawless and without error or contradiction. God's purpose is to communicate to man in a way that it can be understood, right? I studied all three of these systems extensively. In Covenant Theology alone, I spent over three years studying many of their notable theologians like Charles Hodge. Please understand that it is not my intention to berate any Christian's belief system for the Lord God loves us all and wants us to come to the knowledge of the truth. I am sure that on this all of us can agree.

Regardless of the *system*, all that is needed is one failure to justify changing the system or, at least, considering alternatives. Not to do so will make our dedication to the *system* greater than our dedication to the *Word of God*. In the next letter, we will look at our third and final *system of interpretation*.

Trusting in *His Word*,
Dr. David Alan Greene

Chapter 4

To Theophilus:

If you have made it this far, I commend you. I have found that two groups of people cannot be taught. First, there are those who do not want to learn. Since you are reading these letters, you are certainly not part of that group. Second, there are those who already know everything. A closed mind is difficult to open. These good folks mostly read whatever confirms what they already believe. This validates that what they have already been taught is correct. They might find this book to be somewhat of a challenge and, at times, offensive. It may cause some to question their assumptions or beliefs. However, each of us has the free will to believe whatever we wish. The choice is ours to make. As for you, fear not! Personally, I believe you will be pleasantly surprised how plain the Bible becomes; especially concerning the end times!

Anytime we use a *system of interpretation*, we must continually apply the test of truth. Here it is again. First, we must use only one single system. We cannot use multiple systems. This singular system must be applied to the entire Bible from Genesis to Revelation. Second, there can be no failure which is the creation of a conflict in the *Word of God*. Failure is like a smoke detector. Continually applying the test is like keeping fresh batteries in your smoke detectors. I was an insurance agent for over thirty-five years. It is for our safety. When we interpret one portion of Scripture and it conflicts with another, it is enough to make us stop and check our interpretation. That is all. Think about a computer program. The program either works or it does not. If it fails, then the code must be corrected and tested again.

Thus far, we have eliminated the *existential system* because it is not a system. Its interpretation is based upon an individual's whim or fancy. Then, we introduced the *covenant system*. We will continue to examine it when we discuss the *dispensational system*. It is easier to understand when we stop and make comparisons between the two systems. It will be the clearest way for you to see their differences in both their method of application and resulting interpretation.

I mentioned *covenant theology* is perhaps the most prevalent within evangelical churches. *Dispensational Theology* is less common because there are fewer seminaries that teach it. *Covenant Theology* has the Catholic Church and large Protestant denominations which are dedicated to its propagation. You will need to search for an assembly that teaches the Bible dispensationally. Truth is rarely found in popularity. Remember the question I asked earlier. "How many people does it take to make something true?" The correct answer is only One: God!

Some will say that *Covenant Theology* originated with Luther and Calvin. Therefore, it precedes the development of *Dispensational Theology* by theologians like John Nelson Darby, Lewis Sperry Chafer, and Charles Ryrie. All of these writers were from the late 1800s to the present and came after Calvin and Luther. They hold to the concept of progressive theology which means that truth evolves over time. Does truth really change? They would say that it does. Biblical truth does not evolve regardless of whoever or whatever way man decides to interpret it. God and *His Word* never changes!

What would you say if I told you the origin of *Dispensational Theology* came from the first century?

That may raise a few eyebrows. So, who established Dispensational Theology as a tool to interpret the *Word of God?* It was the Apostle Paul. Timothy was a fellow worker learning under Paul's careful instruction. Paul wanted Timothy to teach the *Word of God* correctly. He wrote to him in 2 Timothy 2:15:

15 [Timothy] Study to shew thyself approved unto God, a workman that needeth not to be ashamed, <u>rightly dividing the word of truth</u>.

Paul did not want Timothy to be ashamed or embarrassed by interpreting the Bible incorrectly.

Paul used the Greek word *orthotomeo* which is translated as *rightly dividing.* It is a compound word comprised of *ortho* and *tomeo.* The word *ortho* means *correct* or *with great precision.* As an example, look at the word *orthodox* which is also a compound word. *Ortho* means *correct* and *dox* means *doctrine.* Put together, it means *correct doctrine.* For the word *orthotomeo,* the last part of the word is *tomeo* which means *to cut.* Some may remember a medical procedure called a *tonsillectomy.* It is comprised of three Greek words: *tonsil* plus *ex* which means *out* and *tomeo* which means *to cut.* Unfortunately, the New Age translations lose the integrity of the Greek.

Instead, they translated it as *correctly handle.* Consider this. Would you want a surgeon to remove infected tonsils by *correctly handled* or by *cutting with great precision?*

Paul told Timothy he needs to study the Bible in a way that is approved by God. If it is approved by God, then maybe we should do this too. In order to do it correctly, Timothy must carefully divide God's Word and interpret it accordingly. This applies to the *Word of God* as a whole. The Dispensational Theology is about carefully dividing the Bible. Each division is called a *dispensation.* When we do this correctly, you *will* see things you never saw before. Yet, the Holy Scripture never changed! Our method of observation has. It will be the Holy Spirit Who reveals the *Word of God* to you – *rightly divided!*

Most theologians use another *tool* to interpret the Bible: by literal-historical-grammatical examination of the text. This tool is used by *dispensational theologians* who have a high view of Scripture. Carpenters have a set of tools in their belts. Picture a carpenter carrying under her arm a pine board seven feet long. She is doing a project for a local elementary school teacher. She was asked to cut the board into seven pieces representing the seven days of the week. When it is put together, it is still the same board, right? It has only been divided into seven sections. You now understand the concept of *Dispensational Theology!*

The word *dispensation* has nothing to do with the old meaning of the word. In the Middle Ages, it meant that special permission could be granted to someone for the payment of a fee. For our use, the word means *the act or process of dispensing something.* This would be the same way a court system *dispenses* justice. Don't be alarmed. Many people have never heard the word *dispensation* used in the Bible. It is used exclusively by Paul in his epistles and found in 1 Corinthians 9:17, Ephesians 1:10, and Colossians 1:25. It is also used in Ephesians 3:2:

> **2 If ye have heard of the <u>dispensation</u> of the grace of God which is given me to you-ward [for you]:**

In some of the modern translations, instead of *dispensation* the following alternative words are used: *administration, stewardship,* and the New Living Bible uses *special responsibility.*

The word *dispensation* comes from two Greek words. The first is *oikos* which means *household* and the second is *nomos* which means *law.* This is where our word *economy* (*oikos* + *nomos*). That makes sense as the health of country's economy is dependent upon the dispensing or administering government policy. For our purpose, a *dispensation* will be considered *a period of time in which God dispenses or administrates His household or Creation.* Although dispensations involve time, they are not all equal in length. Some begin and end while others may run concurrently. Each dispensation has a steward or stewards who are appointed by God to oversee His earthly administration.

Think about building a bookcase to organize your books so you can easily access them. A *system* is similar. It is a way of organizing something. Like a proper *tool*, it makes the task easier. This tool does not pose a threat to the Bible or its contents. It is only a way of organizing the Bible. By doing this, it changes our viewpoint. This useful *tool* makes understanding the Bible as a whole and, specifically, the end times so much easier. You can pause for a moment and breathe a sigh of relief. Finally, something is going to make understanding the Bible easier!

Here are some key benefits for us by applying this dispensational tool. You will understand: (1) where we are right now in God's timeline, (2) why certain events are happening now. Finally, (3) how all this will end with the fulfillment of God's divine plan. It is worth the investment of your time when you consider the value of this *tool*. There are many books on how to understand the Bible. Very few apply this *tool* in the same way we will. I will not ask you to join or support any group, send money for a cause, or do anything. A teacher teaches. Beyond that, it is the prerogative of those who learn to apply that knowledge as they choose. The Bible never changes, but it does change the people who understand it.

Our goal now is to gain a greater understanding of *Dispensational Theology*. It is best understood by seeing it applied. As we do this, you will be able to compare it with the views of *Covenant Theology*. We will apply this new *dispensational tool* to the Bible starting in the next letter.

In His service,
Dr. David Alan Greene

Chapter 5

To Theophilus:

We will start by pointing out the major difference between *Dispensational Theology* and *Covenant Theology*. The latter sees the Bible as one long administration. They see God's chosen people, which they call the "Church," as one singular group. In the past, the Jews were God's chosen people. Later, in the New Testament, many Jews rejected their Messiah. As a result of that, new believers which were mostly Gentiles became God's chosen people. They are the present "Church." *Covenant Theology* teaches that those who are saved today are the true "Church."

Dispensational Theology, however, sees the Bible as a series of seven dispensations. In these dispensations, God deals differently with whoever and in whatever manner He so chooses. There is no loss of God's sovereignty. The words *dispensation* and *age*, for our purposes, will be synonymous. We will use them interchangeably. Now, we will start working our way through these seven dispensations.

The doctrinal importance of the book of Genesis cannot be overstated because this one book contains four of the seven dispensations! Therefore, it would be very beneficial for anyone looking to understand these four dispensations to read the book of Genesis. As the different dispensations are presented, read along in the Bible to see the changes as they occur within the text.

The Age of Innocence

The first dispensation begins with the creation of Adam. God made him the steward to care for His Creation. There are three names by which this age is known: the Adamic Age, Edenic Age, or Age of Innocence. We will use the latter. I want to call to your attention one word – *replenish*. It means to *refill*. This word was used when Noah left the Ark following the Great Flood. In the KJV, this word *replenish* is used twice. After the great Flood, God told Noah and his sons to be fruitful, multiply, and *replenish* the earth. (See Genesis 9:1). In similar fashion, God spoke to Adam and Eve. Genesis 1:28:

28 And God blessed them, and God said unto them, Be fruitful, and multiply, and replenish the earth, and subdue it: and have dominion over the fish of the sea, and over the fowl of the air, and over every living thing that moveth upon the earth. Genesis 1:28

Our first dispensation begins with the creation of Adam. However, there is biblical evidence that there were ages that preceded the creation of Adam. It was the Age of Innocence and a new beginning.

There are many dialogs between the Creator and His Creatures recorded in the Bible. They were dictated to Moses on Mount Sinai by a credible eyewitness – the Creator Himself. God gave Adam specific instructions as to what he could not do. The severity of the consequences for his disobedience where repeated.

In Genesis, God chose six days for the Creation and on the seventh day He rested. Known as the Sabbath, this sacred day God called all Creation to rest. To this present day, the Jews continue to observe this as a holy day. It would be a foreshadowing or type for the completion of the seven dispensations. The Age of Innocence begins with the creation of the first man and ends with his subsequent Fall.

Adam and Eve chose to disobey God and the effects of this are far-reaching. God expelled the couple from the Garden of Eden which ends the first dispensation. There was no going back. Note that they could not re-enter paradise because of flaming swords which prevented it. (See Genesis 3:24.) Adam and Eve left paradise and entered a different world. God had pronounced a curse upon them and the earth. Genesis 3:17-19:

> 17 **And unto Adam he said, Because thou hast hearkened unto the voice of thy wife, and hast eaten of the tree, of which I commanded thee, saying, Thou shalt not eat of it: <u>cursed is the ground for thy sake; in sorrow shalt thou eat of it all the days of thy life;</u>**
>
> 18 **<u>Thorns also and thistles shall it bring forth to thee; and thou shalt eat the herb of the field;</u>**
>
> 19 **<u>In the sweat of thy face shalt thou eat bread, till thou return unto the ground; for out of it wast thou taken: for dust thou art, and unto dust shalt thou return.</u>**

From the last verse, notice the words used at many graveside funerals. We are but frail creatures made of clay and quickened by God's breath of life. Our dependency as Creatures must always be upon our Creator, but few are humble enough to accept this.

The Age of Conscience

When the couple left the Garden of Eden, Adam and Eve entered a fallen world. They were naked and afraid. So, the first sacrifice recorded was God preparing coverings for them made with animal skins. It was symbolic. Future sacrifices would also be temporary coverings until the final solution for sin is presented.

God had instilled in the couple a conscience. It is the knowledge of the existence of God and the difference between right and wrong. A conscience is an inherent part of each child. For this reason, it is called the Age of Conscience. They no longer had the presence of God walking with them. Instead, they must rely on their conscience to be their guide. Today, every person has a conscience. They have the knowledge of right and wrong to guide them.

Since having the knowledge of good and evil, man's tendency has always been toward sin. Years passed and the state of mankind deteriorated. God could no longer look upon the state of evil. There were millions of people inhabiting the earth at this time. Jesus referred to this time particular state of humanity when speaking about the end times. The entire chapter of Matthew 24 concerns the tribulation period which will end with His Second Coming. Notice His comparison with this time of Noah (Noe). Matthew 24:37-39:

> 37 **But as the days of Noe were, so shall also the coming of the Son of man be.**
>
> 38 **For as in the days that were before the flood they were eating and drinking, marrying and giving in marriage, until the day that Noe entered into the ark,**
>
> 39 **And knew not until the flood came, and took them all away; so shall also the coming of the Son of man be.**

Notice the state or condition of mankind prior to God's judgement by the Flood. It compares the abrupt and unexpected judgment of the Flood to that of the coming of the Lord Jesus Christ.

Think about the extent of this judgment. Although the Bible does not state the number of people, analysts have estimated the number of people judged. They used the average length of life, the human reproduction rate, and other factors to estimate this number to be between 100 million to 2 billion people. Stop and think about this for a moment. How many of people chose to believe God? This is an important question. They heard Noah preaching repentance for 120 years. Yet, there were only eight people who had believed. Only eight were saved from the Flood: Noah, his three sons, and their wives. All the others chose not reject God's warning. This is one example I use to make a point. Truth is never determined by popularity. *Truth* is never in vogue. It is almost always rejected by the majority! Please take note of this as it is seen repeatedly throughut *God's Word.*

The conscience is present in all humans. This internal guide is often referred to as the Moral Law. Here is a question I get asked a lot when explaining the Bible. "What about all the people who don't believe in Jesus?" This Moral Law, the one everyone receives internally, is important. It will be the basis upon which the consequences of their actions will be determined. The role of Conscience continues to play an important part in the future of mankind. There is the never-ending stream of accusations and judgements which people make against each other. Using their consciences, they make themselves to be like God by judging others.

According to Common Law, once a judgement is made, it becomes precedent upon which all subsequent judgements are made. When those who are not saved judge others, they are, by their own action, establishing the precedent by which they themselves will be judged! See Jesus' warning in Matthew 7:1-5:

> 1 **Judge not, that ye be not judged.** 2 <u>**For with what judgement ye judge, ye shall be judged: and with what measure ye mete, it shall be measured to you again.**</u>
>
> 3 **And why beholdest thou the [speck] mote that is in thy brother's eye, but considerest not the [plank] beam that is in thine own eye?** 4 **Or how wilt thou say to thy brother, Let me pull out the mote out of thine eye; and, behold, a beam is in thine own eye?**
>
> 5 **Thou hypocrite, [instead] first cast out the beam out of thine own eye; and then shalt thou see clearly to [help] cast out the mote [speck] out of thy brother's eye.**

Paul also wrote about the conscience. The Gentiles did not receive the Mosaic Law. Paul explains the conscience to the Gentiles in Romans 2:15:

> 15 **Which shew the work of the [Moral Law] law written in their hearts, <u>their conscience</u> also bearing witness, and their thoughts the mean while [also] <u>accusing or else excusing one another</u> . . .**

That would mean that those who judge others either accuse them or excuse them. In another epistle Paul talks about the consciences of those who hate and continually rebel against God. He says that God sears their conscience. Searing causes them to no longer feel or hear the conscience speaking to them. We read in 1 Timothy 4:1-2:

> 1 **Now the Spirit speaketh expressly, that in the latter times [end times] some shall depart from the faith, giving heed to seducing spirits, and doctrines of devils; 2 Speaking lies in hypocrisy; <u>having their conscience seared with a hot iron;</u>**

For 120 years, Noah preached of the judgement to come. When the day of judgement came, Noah and his family entered the Ark. It was just a normal day in the lives of the people. We read in Matthew 24:38:

> 38 **For as in the days that were before the flood they were eating and drinking, marrying and giving in marriage, until the day that [Noah] Noe entered into the ark,**

The door to the Ark was closed and sealed by God. Then, the torrential rains came. Picture those re-morseful souls outside the ark beating upon its door, but it was too late. It was not long after that there were only the sounds of the wind and the rain.

It will be two thousand years in 2030, since the Lord Jesus Christ was crucified, buried, and rose again. Salvation has been preached continually since the apostles first carried their messages. I believe there are far fewer people saved than most Christians think. Truth is never popular until it is too late.

Age of Human Government

Following the Flood, the physical state of the world had changed again. The waters had receded and the eight living souls walked out of the Ark. Genesis 9:1-3:

1 And God blessed Noah and his sons, and said unto them, <u>Be fruitful, and multiply, and replenish the earth.</u>

2 And the fear of you and the dread of you shall be upon every beast of the earth, and upon every fowl of the air, upon all that moveth upon the earth, and upon all the fishes of the sea; into your hand are they delivered.

3 Every moving thing that liveth shall be meat for you; even as the green herb have I given you all things.

They were given domain over creation with the exclusion of eating meat with the blood of life still in it. God also instituted capital punishment. Verses 6-7:

6 Whoso [Whoever] sheddeth man's blood, by man shall his blood be shed: for in the image of God made he man.

7 And you, be ye fruitful, and multiply; bring forth abundantly in the earth, and multiply therein.

God blessed Noah and his sons and told them to be fruitful and multiply. They were instructed to refill or cover the earth. However, contrary to God's wishes, they chose to come together to form the first city of Babel. The population exploded again. There was a heavy influence from astrologers who sought information or knowledge from the stars. Later, we will learn about the powers, principalities, and rulers of darkness. Astrology later became a forbidden practices for Israel because the source of that knowledge was not from God.

This dispensation is called the Age of Human Government. All the people had one language and a "collective unity" until they were scattered. Today, the internet in connecting the world in a process of homogenizing all the peoples into a singular collective unity again.

The people of the past built a high tower reaching to the heavens. The name of it was the Tower of Babel. God saw how mankind had come together to seek their own advancement all the while rejecting their Creator. They sought knowledge elsewhere. God's response was to scatter the people into different *tribes*. That work is used today in political speech. He confused their languages and, thus, the *Nations* were created. They still exist. They formed a union to represent mankind's combined interest by uniting the *Nations*. These *United Nations*, or in Hebrew

Goyim, play a critical role in the end times. These nations, also called *the Gentiles,* will be the ones who rebel against God. In a final battle, they will attempt to destroy true Israel who is God's chosen people.

God is always in control. He allows certain choices to be made, but He remains sovereign. Paul assures us, "For there is no power but of God: the powers that be are ordained of God" (Rom. 13:1). It is God's intent that the human conscience and human government continue until this final battle.

The Age of Promise

These scattered people formed the *Nations* and, out of these nations, God called one man – Abraham. God made a covenant with him and this promise. Genesis 12:1-2:

> 1 **Now the LORD had said unto Abram, Get thee out of thy country, and from thy kindred, and from thy father's house, unto a land that I will shew thee:**
>
> 2 **And <u>I will make of thee a great nation, and I will bless thee, and make thy name great; and thou shalt be a blessing:</u>**

Abram came from the land of Ur which was in present-day Iraq. The next verse speaks of Israel's friends and enemies. This applies not only to the past and present, but it applies to those *Nations* during the end times. At that time, God will separate those who blessed Abraham's descendants from those who cursed them. This applies particularly during the Tribulation. Their actions towards Israel will have eternal consequences. Verse 3:

> 3 **And I will bless them that bless thee, and curse him that curseth thee: and in thee shall all families of the earth be blessed.**

Covenant Theologians refer to this *calling out* of Abraham. They teach that God's chosen – the "Church" – started here. Notice in the covenant that God used the pronoun *thee* in referring to Abraham. The word *thee* is the singular form of the pronoun *you*. It is important to see that this promise was made to Abraham and, through him, to his descendants. Covenants and promises by God are eternal and will continue. This is the fourth and last dispensation to be found in Genesis. This is known as the *Abrahamic Age* or the *Age of Promise*.

It was God Who divided. There are now two groups of people which will continue until the end times. They are the *Children of Abraham* whom God appointed to serve Him. They are known as the Jews. Then, there is everyone else. They are the non-Jews. Let us stop for a moment and think about the end times. The *Nations,* wishing to destroy God's chosen people, come together once again. In the great battle, they join forces to eliminate Israel – God's chosen, the *Children of Abraham!*

Before we leave the book of Genesis, I would like us to think about the word *seed.* The singular or plural of the word *seed* is the same. When we think about the *seed* of Abraham, most believe it refers to the descendants of Abraham collectively. What if it refers to the Promised Seed Who is Jesus Christ? In Matthew 1, it begins with the geneaology of Jesus Christ. There we learn that He is the Son of Adam later called the Son of Man. He is the Son of David. Most importantly, we see that Jesus Christ is also *the Seed* – the Son of Abraham.

Teaching the *Word of God,*
Dr. David Alan Greene

Chapter 6

Theophilus,

The first dispensation, the *Age of Innocence*, ended with the expulsion from the Garden of Eden. There is no returning to that state or location until all has been made righteous and sin has been irradicated. The *Age of Conscience* continues in all mankind with their inherent nature including a conscience or, as some may call it, the knowledge of God and right-and-wrong.

The dispensation of *Human Government* continues. God instituted government with the power of capital punishment. Governments have far exceeded God's intent and continue to grow in size and power. Each nation has its own land and many have a unique language. From one large homogenous group, God created many which explains cultural or tribal diversity. When we look at the current state of consolidating countries, are they not working their way back to their original state at the Tower of Babel?

Out of this multitude of nations, God called one man – Abraham. God had plans for him and his descendants. The Abrahamic Covenant required a physical mark. All males are circumcised as a sign of this covenant. As a group, they will be known as *the Circumcision.* That will become more important later in understanding how God deals with the *Circumcision* differently than He deals with the *Uncircumcision* or the Gentiles.

The story of Joseph is referred to as a typology because it is representative of something in the future. Joseph was rejected by his brothers because he was much loved by his father Jacob. Joseph, as a *type,* represents the future Savior because he saves or redeems his brothers. The first time that the brothers see Joseph, they do not recognize him. The first time the Messiah appeared, the Jews did not recognize Him either. However, the second time they do recognize Joseph and share in a joyous restoration. So too will the reunion be when the Messiah returns to save Israel in the end.

The Bible continues to record the history of Abraham's children. Joseph was second in command in Egypt and a brilliant administrator over Pharoah's kingdom. The Jewish people thrived and grew in number as God blessed them. Exodus 1:7-8:

7 And the children of Israel were fruitful, and increased abundantly, and mul-
tiplied, and waxed [grew] exceeding
mighty; and the land was filled with
them.

8 Now there arose up a new king over
Egypt, which knew not Joseph.

When a new Pharoah came to power, the Jewish people suddenly found themselves in a dire state. This
new Pharoah "knew not Joseph." God heard their
cries and chose a man named Moses to "save" them
as they had become slaves. Moses was also a *type* or
example of the Savior Who will save His people.
Genesis and Exodus are two wonderful books and
definitely worth the read. These two books provide
an understanding of the remainder of the Bible. They
are written in a narrative style and are told as stories.
We must confine ourselves to only the major points
for our purpose. Be sure to read them!

Moses is famous for uttering the words of God,
"Let My people go!" Exodus records the complete
defeat of Pharoah and his army. Freed from their op-
pressive state, Moses leads them towards the land
promised to Abraham in Genesis 15:18:

18 In the same day the LORD made a covenant with Abram, saying, Unto thy seed have I given this land, from the river of Egypt unto the great river, the river Euphrates:

This is the Promised Land – another promise God made to Abraham. It is the ultimate destination of the children of Israel. Exodus 3:8:

8 And I am come down to deliver them out of the hand of the Egyptians, and <u>to bring them up out of that land unto a good land and a large, unto a land flowing with milk and honey</u> . . .

In the Wilderness, God made them into a holy nation. The word *holy* means *separated unto God*. This involved a legal agreement referred to as a *Suzerain and Vassal Covenant*. This type of agreement was unique because it involved a super, powerful ruler called a Suzerain and a dependent, weaker party called the Vassal. This type of agreement was prevalent among other nations at this time. It is the ratification of this agreement that moves us into the next dispensation.

The Age of Law

The Abrahamic Covenant was unilateral agreement meaning that the responsibility for fulfillment would be borne by one party – God. However, the Mosaic Covenant is a bilateral agreement which obligates both parties. Also, the *Suzerain and Vassal Covenant* is conditional. Each party must agree to abide by the terms and conditions. They must fulfill the conditions or face the penalties outlined in the agreement. We will spend some time examining this as it becomes the primary controlling factor for Israel from this point forward.

The Suzerain is a powerful king who has abundant resources and power. He comes to the aid of the Vassal state who is weaker and unable to defend itself against another great power. Such is the case when God triumphantly brought the children of Israel out from under the yoke of Pharoah. By agreeing to the Covenant, Israel, the Vassal state, was required to promise allegiance to God, their Suzerain. Their benefits included protection and provisions from the Suzerain, but there were certain obligations. Penalties would be applied for breach of contract. This would apply immediately. The situation in which they found themselves in the Wilderness made them completely dependent upon God.

By a miraculous act of God Almighty, Israel was saved from certain defeat by its formidable enemy. God victoriously destroyed Pharoah and his entire army. However, their need for dependence and protection continued. Acting in the role of a Suzerain, God put forth to them an agreement using Moses as His intermediary. God directed Moses to bring His offer to the people in Exodus 19:4-6:

> **4 Ye have seen what I did unto the Egyptians, and how I bare you on eagles' wings, and brought you unto myself.**
>
> **5 Now therefore, if ye will obey my voice indeed, and keep my covenant, then ye shall be a peculiar treasure unto me above all people: for all the earth is mine:**
>
> **6 <u>And ye shall be unto me a kingdom of priests, and an holy nation.</u> These are the words which thou shalt speak unto the children of Israel.**

The word *peculiar* means *to be uniquely different from all others.* The word *holy* does not mean to be perfect, but instead means *to be separated from.* Notice the purpose of the covenant. They are to be a *separate nation dedicated to God.* Someday, Israel will act as intermediaries between God and the other nations. As such, they will play a prominent role in the establishment of the future Kingdom and restoration of Creation.

The Mosaic Covenant is a two-party bilateral contract. Therefore, both parties must agree to and abide by the terms and conditions. Verses 7-8:

> 7 **And Moses came and called for the elders of the people, and <u>laid before their faces all these words which the LORD commanded him.</u>**

> 8 **And all the people answered together, and said, <u>All that the LORD hath spoken we will do. And Moses returned the words of the people unto the LORD.</u>**

Moses returned the response from the people to God signifying their acceptance of His terms. This made the Mosaic Covenant an everlasting covenant – a binding agreement between the two parties.

The agreement included what is referred to as *the blessings and the curses.* These are conditional. If the agreement is followed, there are blessings. If the agreement is broken, there are penalties. Later, we will see the results. God punishes Israel for failing to keep the requirements. Here is the interesting part.

Breaking just one point is as bad as breaking all of them. We read about this in Deuteronomy 27:1:

> 1 **And Moses with the elders of Israel commanded the people, saying, <u>Keep all the commandments which I command you</u> this day.**

Did you see the words *all* the commandments? That means they cannot miss or fall short on one point! Imagine how difficult that would be for anyone to keep *all* of the Law without exception! Now consider this. It would take a very special Someone to fulfill all the Law. That Someone would then be without spot or blemish. Our own human nature is sinful because of Adam's original sin. That sin nature is transmitted by the male and not the female. Yet, Jesus had a human mother, Mary. Joseph was not His biological father. It was the Holy Spirit Who caused Mary to conceive and bear a Son. Therefore, Jesus' Father was not a man but God Himself. Since God created Adam, He could certainly handle the details of creating a baby within Mary's womb.

After the resurrection, the Apostle James was writing his epistle addressed "to the twelve tribes which are scattered abroad" (Jas. 1:1). His letter was sent to the remnant of Jews. In it, he confirms that the requirements of the Mosaic Covenant have not changed. They remain in full effect for the children of Abraham. James 2:10:

> 10 **For whosoever shall keep the whole law, and yet [but] <u>offend in one point, he is guilty of all</u>.**

At the same time that the Mosaic Law was instituted, God also established the Levitical Priesthood. They would intercede between God and the people and offer sacrifices to appease God's anger *temporarily covering* Israel's sins. We will find that Israel's sins will not be forgiven until the end times.

God told Moses before he died that the people would abandon their love for God. Exodus 31:16:

> 16 **And the LORD said unto Moses, Behold, thou shalt sleep with thy fathers; and <u>this people will rise up, and go a whoring after the gods of the strangers of the land, whither they go to be among them, and will forsake me, and break my covenant which I have made with them</u>.**

When they do that, what will God's response be? Verse 17:

17 Then my anger shall be kindled against them in that day, and I will forsake them, and I will hide my face from them, and they shall be devoured, and many evils and troubles shall befall them; so that they will say in that day, Are not these evils come upon us, because our God is not among us?

As a result, they were in Egypt for 400 years. Eventually, God would bring them back to the land because <u>He had promised their fathers</u>. You will see those words again later. Below, it is referred to as the land *that flows with milk and honey.* God knew they would abandon Him and speaks of the consequences of their actions in Deuteronomy 31:20:

20 For when I shall have brought them into the land which I sware unto their fathers, that floweth with milk and honey; and they shall have eaten and filled themselves, and waxen fat; then will they turn unto other gods, and serve them, and provoke me, and break my covenant.

God knows that after they arrive in the Promised Land and are filled with its goodness, they will once again break His covenant.

66

The *Mosaic Age* is the fifth dispensation of the seven. It is clear to see that Moses was God's administrator or steward during this dispensation. This administration continues through the remainder of the Old Testament as well as up to and including Jesus's earthly ministry. What was Jesus' view on the Mosaic Law? The Gospel of Matthew records His own words in verses 5:17-18:

> 17 **Think not that I am come to destroy the law, or the prophets: <u>I am not come to destroy, but to fulfil.</u>**
>
> 18 **For verily I say unto you, Till heaven and earth pass, <u>one jot or one tittle shall in no wise pass from the law, till all be fulfilled.</u>**

This covenant is permanent. Think about this. Jesus is talking about the Law being *fulfilled!* How is that humanly possible? Maybe the answer is within the question. It isn't. It would take Someone who is very special, Someone Who is perfect, to *fulfill* the Law!

I look forward to writing my next letter.

Loving the *Word of God,*
Dr. David Alan Greene

Chapter 7

To Theophilus:

I would like to commend you for your perseverance. To understand the end times, we must understand the Bible as a whole. How the Bible is laid out with different dispensations is the key. To know for sure, we must be able to support our conclusions with biblical evidence and it must pass the test of truth. The end God achieves His plan to restore His fallen Creation. Therefore, we must see His plan as it develops. Dispensations are like building blocks in which God advances His purpose towards that end.

God made covenants and promises, but He also gave prophecies. All of these, He must keep because of Who He is. The Old Testament is a wonderful source of information to achieve our goal of understanding the end times. Without it, we are left guessing and there is no confidence in that. We must use biblical facts to support our conclusions.

There is so much history recorded in the Old Testament. However, due to space limitations, we will only be summarizing the major points. I want to encourage you to return to any portion discussed here and read it within its context. Once we can see the entire framework by which the Bible was constructed, we will understand all the pieces. This includes the end times.

Here is a summary of the nation Israel's history. It is best described as a continuous cycle. They receive God's blessing and favor. This is followed by a falling away from God and breaking their Covenant. As a result, they suffer judgement by God. Ultimately, this leads to Israel's repentance and restoration. Suffering these judgements, Israel eventually repents and turns back to God. When they do, they are restored and, once again, receive God's blessing. You will find this cycle repeating continually throughout the Old Testament as they wait for their Messiah.

Let us go back to Moses briefly. Before his death, God anointed Joshua as his replacement. I would like to give another example of how numbers never indicate or prove truth. There were an estimated 2.5 million children of Israel who were brought out of Egypt. Of these, there were an estimated 600,000 adult males. How many of these men reached the Promised Land? The answer is only two. They were Joshua and Caleb. Why? These two men had faith. They *believed* God. Previously, we learned about Abraham, "And he *believed* in the LORD; and He counted it to him for righteousness" (Gen. 15:5-6). Wait a second. There seems to be a theme developing here! It looks like *believing* or *having faith* in what God says is the key!

After Joshua, there was a brief period of Judges ruling over the twelve tribes like local magistrates. Then, the tribes noticed the surrounding nations had kings. So, Israel wanted a king too. They chose for themselves their first king who was Saul, a warrior. This did not end well. So, God appointed King David to be Saul's successor and God blessed him. Under his leadership, David conquered Jerusalem and unified the twelve tribes into the Davidic Kingdom. This will be sufficient to provide the background for our purpose. We will now focus on the covenant God made with King David because it concerns the future of the Davidic Kingdom.

The story of this covenant is found in 2 Samuel 7. It is also mentioned several times in the books of Chronicles. Similar to the Abrahamic Covenant, the Davidic Covenant is also unconditional. Its fulfillment is totally dependent upon God. It is called the Davidic Covenant or the Davidic Promise. This agreement was made between God and David, the King of Israel. It promises the establishment of an everlasting Kingdom to be fulfilled by David's son and heir to his throne.

Let us look at the context of this promise. We will see shortly how this relates to God's future plan. Notice the use of the future tense in the following text. 2 Samuel 7:10-11:

> 10 Moreover <u>I will</u> appoint a place for my people Israel, and <u>will</u> plant them, that they may dwell in a place of their own, and move no more; neither <u>shall</u> the children of wickedness afflict them any more, as beforetime,
>
> 11 And as since the time that I commanded judges to be over my people Israel, and have caused thee to rest from all thine enemies. Also the LORD telleth thee that he <u>will</u> make thee [David] an house [dynasty].

He used words like "I will" to signify a future event. This is prophetic because it concerns something that "will" take place in the future.

He continues addressing King David in verse 12:

12 And [David] when thy days be ful-filled, and thou shalt sleep with thy fathers, <u>I will</u> set up thy seed after thee, which <u>shall</u> proceed out of thy bowels [body], and <u>I will</u> establish his kingdom.

This reference is to the future King Who would be a direct descendent of King David. Notice the use of the word "seed." This Seed is Jesus Christ. He will be the Son of David Who will establish David's Kingdom forever! He continues by speaking about this coming King. Verses 13-16:

13 He <u>shall build</u> an house for my name, and I [God] <u>will stablish</u> the throne of his kingdom for ever.

14 I <u>will be</u> his father, and he <u>shall be</u> my son. If he commit iniquity, I will chasten him with the rod of men, and with the stripes of the children of men:

15 But my mercy <u>shall</u> not depart away from him, as I took it from Saul, whom I put away before thee. 16 And thine

**house and thy kingdom <u>shall be estab-
lished for ever</u> before thee: thy throne
<u>shall be established for ever.</u>**

Clearly, we can see the importance of this Kingdom.
It will be ruled by Israel's eternal King. His throne
will be established forever. Israel was "called-out" to
be a holy nation of priests who will serve their eternal King.

Many people believed it was David's son Solomon who would fulfill this promise. That was not the
case. Solomon began to marry foreign women and
worship their foreign gods. God was not pleased! He
did not punish Solomon because of His relationship
with David. However, following Solomon's death,
the Kingdom was divided. Solomon had two sons:
Rehoboam and Jeroboam. The latter revolted and
fought against his brother. Ultimately, the Kingdom
was divided. The two tribes of Benjamin and Judah
remained under Rehoboam, the rightful king. Its
capital was in Jerusalem. They are referred to as *Judah*. The northern ten tribes followed Jeroboam as
their king. They established their capital in Samaria.
This group is referred to as *Israel* or the northern
kingdom. This will be important later when we see
how God uses the names of Israel and Judah.

The history of the northern kingdom was short. They followed after false gods. After repeated warnings, God brought judgement. The Assyrians who were a mighty warring nation came, defeated, and carried the ten tribes off into captivity. They used a tactic of assimilation to mix these Jews into their own people. Some returned to dwell in the northern region were called Samaritans. They were considered by the Jews to be half-breeds and, therefore, not Jewish. The term *Jew* was derived from the tribe of *Judah*. The name Judah includes both the tribes of Judah and Benjamin. This brings a greater meaning to how lowly and despised the Samaritan were when Jesus told the parable of the Good Samaritan. (See Luke 10:25-37.) It was not the righteous Jew but the lowly Samaritan who exercised mercy.

The Davidic Promise of the eternal Heir to David's throne was always in the minds of the Jews. It was their hope and reassurance that God would preserve His holy nation. This resonated especially during the Roman occupation. Their expectations of a mighty warrior-king coming to save them from their oppressors was premature. It will happen, but not until later. God must first accomplish His other objectives. First and foremost in the minds of the Jews were the coming King and David's eternal Kingdom.

If we go to the very beginning of the Gospel of Matthew, then you will see the significance of what we just discussed. The first chapter of the first book in the New Testament is dedicated to the genealogy of Jesus Christ. It is intended to establish, without any doubt, Jesus' rightful claim to David's throne. Verse 1:

> 1 **The book of the generation of Jesus Christ, <u>the son of David</u>, <u>the son of Abraham</u>.**

Here we have confirmation that Jesus is the direct descendant of both Abraham, making Jesus the *Seed of Abraham,* as well as the *Son of David.* We have written proof that Jesus Christ is the legitimate Heir to the throne of Israel. It is for that reason many Jews in the gospels call Jesus the *Son of David.* They were fully aware of the prophecy God gave to King David.

The ten northern tribes, collectively known, as Israel, were carried off by the Assyrians in approximately 722 B.C. Because of the assimilation, these ten tribes are often referred to as the ten lost tribes of Israel. The two remaining tribes of Benjamin and Judah continued to operate the temple sacrifices in Jerusalem. similar to its northern cousins, they also began worshipping false gods and idols. God sent them prophets warning them of judgement if they did not repent. They ignored God's messengers, the prophets, and continued to disobey Him. This resulted in what is called the *Babylonian Exile* or *Babylonian Captivity*. Most Christians have heard the stories of Daniel in the Bible like Daniel in the Lion's Den and Daniel in the Fiery Furnace. He was one of the young princes carried off by King Nebuchadnezzar's army to Babylon.

God protected Daniel and blessed him. The Babylonian king saw this and favored him. The entire book of Daniel records the history of this faithful young man. Daniel became the king's most trusted advisor. The book of Daniel is an important key to understanding the end times! I was teaching a men's Bible class on Revelation. The first night, I asked how many of them wanted to understand the end times. Everyone did. Great! Then, I told them to turn to the book of Daniel. I told them that if they wanted to understand Revelation and the end times, then the book of Daniel was the key. Initially, they were hesitant, but they later agreed. I am confident you will find my next letter interesting!

Honoring the *Word of God,*
Dr. David Alan Greene

Chapter 8

To Theophilus:

The two remaining tribes, known collectively as Judah, were defeated by the Babylonian armies. God allowed this because they had broken the Mosaic Covenant. Yet, under God's protection, they were not killed, but taken into captivity about 586 B.C. They were taken to Babylon the capital of Nebuchadnezzar's Empire. This left Jerusalem destroyed and utterly desolate. This captivity would last seventy years. Why? The Jews had failed, according to the Mosaic Law, to observe the required Sabbath years. This resulted in the seventy-year punishment.

The book of Daniel provides the story of young Daniel's trials and tribulations as well as his rise to prominence in the government. Written in the narrative style the book is easy to read with the exception of the prophecies. For our purpose, we are going to focus our attention on one particular prophecy. This will provide us with a valuable timeline that will make understanding the end times clearer. The Jews remain under the Mosaic Law. The Babylonian Captivity resulted from breaking the Mosaic Law. It fulfilled the prophecy God gave to Moses just before he died. The Lord told him, ". . . this people . . . will forsake me, and break my covenant which I have made with them" (Ex. 19:16). All twelve tribes had turned away from God. Two of them were now in exile.

Daniel was a great man of faith. God elevated him to a prominent position in King Nebuchadnezzar's palace. After a time, news reached Daniel from caravans that Jerusalem was in a terrible state. Daniel admitted to God that the people were not worthy. He asks God to consider Jerusalem because it is known by the Nations as the City of God. Daniel asked God when He will restore the City of Jerusalem.

Upon hearing Daniel's request, God immediately dispatches his angel Gabriel with a response. However, Gabriel is delayed twenty-one days because he was in a spiritual battle with the prince of Persia. The Apostle Paul tells us, "For we wrestle not against flesh and blood, but against principalities, against powers, against the rulers of the darkness of this world, against spiritual wickedness in high places" (Eph. 6:12). The following is an example of this spiritual warfare. Here is the explanation for the delay to Daniel's request. Verse 10:13:

> 13 **But the prince of the kingdom of Persia withstood me one and twenty days: but, lo, Michael, one of the chief princes, came to help me; and I remained there with the kings of Persia.**

As an aside, we learn from this verse that there are spiritual powers ruling over countries and regions. These *powers and principalities* work their evil in the world both then and now under Satan who is "the god of this world" (2 Cor. 4:40. This makes sense when we see what is happening in our world today. There is good news. God will win.

Gabriel finally arrives with God's answer to Daniel's question, but we find it far exceeds the scope of his original request. Daniel 9:24:

> 24 **Seventy weeks are determined upon thy people [the Jews] and upon thy holy city [Jerusalem], to finish the transgression, and to make an end of sins, and to make reconciliation for iniquity, and to bring in everlasting righteousness, and to seal up [complete] the vision and prophecy, and to anoint the most Holy.**

The name *The Most Holy* refers to the Anointed One Who will be anointed as the eternal King.

There is far more going on here than just the physical restoration of Jerusalem. Let us put what God is saying He *will do* into a list. We will refer to it again later. God tells Daniel He will accomplish all of the following by the end of 490 years:

(1) finish transgression, which is sin,
(2) make an end of sin completely,
(3) make a reconciliation for iniquity, which is payment in full for sin,
(4) bring in everlasting righteousness,
(5) seal up, or fulfill, the prophecies, and
(6) anoint the Most Holy.

You can create your own list, but this is my own version. The Most Holy refers to Jesus Christ Whom God will anoint as King. So, God's response speaks about the restoration of Jerusalem, but also the establishment of the eternal Kingdom promised to King David. God has given Daniel a timeline! Yes, God will restore Jerusalem, but He reveals so much more. God *will* establish the Kingdom when He anoints Israel's eternal King – the Lord Jesus Christ, Son of Abraham, Son of David, and Son of God! This is wonderful news. Now, let us decipher the timeline.

Gabriel begins the announcement with the words *seventy weeks*. This is an indication of time. The exile in Babylon was to last seventy years. Here, we find the number seventy mentioned again. However, as we will see in a moment, the seventy weeks actually refers to seventy weeks-of-years. Using simple multiplication, seventy weeks of seven years would total 490 years. Hold that number in your mind.

Gabriel wants to make sure that Daniel understands this fully so he can write it down. So, he breaks down the 490 years by plotting certain events that will occur during this timeline. The majority of Christians and, for that matter, preachers know about this. God created a timeline. Eyebrows raised! We could call it "the Final Countdown." The end times *will* see the fulfillment of all six items listed above. This timeline is the key to understanding the end times. The completion of 490 years will fulfill the promises made to Abraham and King David. With that, let us continue with verse 25:

> 25 **Know therefore and understand, that from the going forth of the commandment to restore and to build Jerusalem unto the Messiah the Prince [comes] shall be seven weeks, and threescore and two weeks: the street shall be built**

again, and the wall, even [that is to say] in troublous times.

God made King Artaxerxes, the successor to King Nebuchadnezzar, favorable towards the Jews. He issued a decree in the seventh year of his reign (Ezra 7:8). There were actually three decrees made over a period of time, but the important decree is the one used by Nehemiah to *rebuild the city walls* of Jerusalem. A city is not a city without its walls. This decree can be accurately dated to 458 B.C.

We will need to do some addition after we look at the first portion of verse 26:

26 **And after threescore and two weeks shall Messiah be cut off, but not for himself . . .**

If we add up seven plus sixty plus two, then the sum is sixty-nine weeks-of-years or 483 years. Gabriel is speaking of the Messiah being *cut off*. As we know the Messiah, the Lord Jesus Christ, was crucified. He was *cut off* by those to whom He was sent. Later on, we will see how the dating of the crucifixion will confirm the accuracy of this prophecy. For now, we need to continue. Verse 26:

. . . and the people of the prince that shall come shall destroy the city and the sanctuary; and the end thereof shall be with a flood, and unto the end of the war desolations are determined.

We need to stop here for a moment. Look at one particular word as it is important. The word is *and*. It is just a conjunction, right? Yes, but it is much more. Sometimes the word *and* signals a break in time. It does not necessarily mean concurrent or immediately consecutive events. Sometimes, when it is used, it denotes a lapse in time. Let us consider the following sentence. Susan was born in London and raised her children in Boston. These two statements are joined together with *and* because *she* is the subject of both actions, but these actions did not occur simultaneously. There was a time span between them.

Now, let us consider an example from the Bible. Following His forty days of testing in the wilderness, Jesus visited the synagogue in Nazareth. It was the official beginning of His earthly ministry and He is about to make an important public proclamation to the Jews. He was called to the bema to read from the Scroll. Luke 4:17-20

17 **And there was delivered unto him the book of the prophet Esaias. And when**

he had opened the book, he found the place where it was written,

18 **The Spirit of the Lord is upon me, because he hath anointed me to preach the gospel to the poor; he hath sent me to heal the brokenhearted, to preach deliverance to the captives, and recovering of sight to the blind, to set at liberty them that are bruised,**

19 **To preach the acceptable year of the Lord. 20 And he closed the book, and he gave it again to the minister, and sat down. And the eyes of all them that were in the synagogue were fastened on him.**

Why were all eyes fastened upon Him? Is this the local boy who has returned home? No! The Jews knew their Scripture! He read from Isaiah 61:1-2. However, Jesus stopped in the middle of verse 2 just before the word *and.* Then, He ended His reading and went to sit down. Verse 21:

21 And he [said] began to say unto them, This day is this scripture fulfilled in your ears.

Jesus read only the first portion of the prophecy. Then, He makes a public proclamation on God's behalf announcing that this portion of the prophecy had been fulfilled in their hearing! He says nothing of the second portion of the prophecy. Why? It will take place at a later time. When? It will occur at the end times. Here is the remainder of Isaiah 61:2:

> ... and the day of vengeance of our God;
> to comfort all that mourn;

Does that sound like the end times to you? So, the judgement portion of this prophecy will occur later during the remaining seven years – the Tribulation. The wrath of God will be released upon His enemies and that will be "the day of vengeance of our God."

So too does the use of the word *and* in Daniel's prophecy represents an unspecified break in time. We will see the cause of this break later, but for now, let us return to Daniel 9:26:

> 26 And after threescore and two weeks shall Messiah be cut off, but not for himself: and [later] the people of the prince that shall come [and] shall destroy the city and the sanctuary; and the end thereof shall be with a flood, and

unto the end of the war desolations are determined.

Following the word *and,* the prophecy speaks about a *future event.* It refers to *the people of the prince.* Who is this *prince?* Previously, I mentioned the "powers, principalities, and rulers of darkness." We will see that "the prince" is also of this spiritual realm. The Apostle Paul referred to him as "the prince of the power of the air, the spirit that now worketh in the children of disobedience" (Eph. 2:2). This is the Antichrist. His actions prove that he could not be the Christ. These *people of the prince* are those who have sworn allegiance to the Antichrist. They belong to him. In the future, there will be multitudes who choose to reject God and follow the Antichrist. Therefore, the *flood* spoken of here is not water. It is a flood of people descending upon Jerusalem to fight God's people until the end of the war of desolations, This word *desolation* means *the act of desolating, destroying, or driving out the inhabitants; ruining; wasting or corrupting.*

Picture sports fans flooding onto a soccer field after a game. It looks like they are pouring onto the field. Millions of people will be deluded by lies. Jesus tells us that Satan is the father of lies and his followers will do their father's bidding. John 8:44:

44 Ye are of your father the devil, and the lusts of your father ye will do. He was a murderer from the beginning, and abode not in the truth, because there is no truth in him. When he speaketh a lie, he speaketh of his own: for he is a liar, and the father of it.

In the future, there will be many lies propagated and, as we know, Satan is the father of lies. This *flood of people* who teach that wrong it right belongs to the Antichrist. They are even marked as his possessions and are those who will *come and destroy the city and the sanctuary* which is the Temple.

In the next verse, the pronoun *he* refers back to the *prince* who is the Antichrist. Here is the first portion of Daniel 9:27:

27 And he shall confirm the covenant with many for one week . . .

Therefore, at the beginning of the seventieth week, the seven last years, the Antichrist creates a global peace accord or *covenant.* I believe the Antichrist has an ulterior motive for doing this. It will motivate all the Jews to return to their homeland. They will joyously rebuild the Temple and resume their offerings or oblations to God. Then, something dire happens halfway through these seven years. Let us read the remainder of verse 27:

> **... and in the midst of the week he shall cause the sacrifice and the oblation to cease and for the overspreading of abominations he shall make it desolate, even [that is to say] until the consummation, and that determined shall be poured upon the desolate.**

Again, the word *and* signifies a break in time. The seven-year covenant begins and, three and one-half years into it, the Antichrist breaks the covenant!

Paul called the Antichrist the Son of Perdition, which means Sin. 2 Thessalonians 2:4:

> **4 Who opposeth [God] and exalteth himself [Antichrist] above all that is called God, or that is worshipped; so that he [Antichrist acting] as God sitteth in the temple of God, shewing himself that he [the Antichrist] is God.**

The word *consummation* means *the ultimate fulfillment or end.* There are three and one-half years remaining which will be much worse than the first half. These are referred to as *the Great Tribulation*. Details of this can be found in the book of Revelation starting with verse 13:5. There you will see the time is broken into two periods of forty-two months which are the same as three and one-half years. In other references, you might see 1260 days referring to the same timeframe. This based upon the Jewish calendar which has 360 days per year.

The bowls and vials are various means of God's "dispensing" of judgement. God will send two witnesses to preach repentance to the people. Some believe that they will be Moses and Elijah. These witnesses will be killed by the people of the prince. There will be 144000 men sent to preach salvation. They too will be murdered. All the details may be interesting. However, for our purpose, we must continue.

How does Daniel's prophetic timeline agree with any real events so far? There is an excellent book written by Sir Robert Anderson entitled *The Coming Prince –The Marvelous Prophecy of Daniel's Seventy Weeks Concerning The Antichrist*. It is a long title, but the book is well worth the read. It goes into great detail on this subject. Let us start with simple arithmetic. So far, we learned that there is a total of 490 years allotted to the consummation. It begins at the date of the decree made by King Artaxerxes in 453 B.C. to rebuild the city walls You might ask, "It has been more than 490 years since that decree. So, what happened?" That is an excellent question and we will provide you with the answer shortly.

There will be 483 years from the date of the decree until the Messiah is cut off. If we deduct 453 from 483 subtract, then we find the difference is 30 years. (Remember to allow for B.C. to A.D.) That makes the date of the crucifixion 30 A.D. Most theologians agree with this date. As a fact check, I like to use the date of the destruction of Jerusalem in 70 A.D. to confirm this. If 30 A.D. is correct, and I believe it is, then it was exactly forty years after the crucifixion of their Messiah that Jerusalem was utterly destroyed by the Roman General Titus. Leaving Jerusalem on Palm Sunday, the disciples commented on the beauty of the city as it neared sundown. Here is Jesus' response to them concerning Jerusalem, "There shall not be left here one stone upon another, that shall not be thrown down" (Matt 24:2). For me, this was sufficient to confirm the accuracy of the first portion of Daniel's prophecy. You may need more proof and there is more proof to come. However, what happened to the remaining seven years? Oh, something definitely happened.

Let us look again at Isaiah 61:2:

2 [1] To proclaim the acceptable year of the LORD, and [2] the day of vengeance of our God; to comfort all that mourn;

Jesus made it clear by His declaration that the bridegroom was with them and rejoicing was in order. The other event was separated by the word *and.* The period of time that separates these two events is unspecified. Something stopped the timeclock. There remains in abeyance the seven remaining years on the Final Countdown. The answer will be made plain shortly.

Next, we will continue to apply the dispensational *tool* to the remainder of the Bible. By doing so, you can plainly see what caused the suspension.

Exalting the *Word of God,*
Dr. David Alan Greene

Chapter 9

To Theophilus:

The beginning of the New Testament is really a continuation of the Old Testament. Dispensationally, it is still part of the Age of Law. All Jews, including Jesus, are under the Mosaic Covenant. Here are Jesus' words affirming that He is changing nothing. Matthew 5:17-18:

> 17 **Think not that I am come to destroy the law, or the prophets: I am not come to destroy, but to fulfil.**
>
> 18 **For verily I say unto you, Till heaven and earth pass, one jot or one tittle shall in no wise pass from the law, till all be fulfilled.**

To be a righteous Man under the Law, God requires every point of the Law be meticulously observed. The Lord Jesus Christ was able to fulfill all the requirements of the Law. He was a righteousness Man. Having accomplished this, God is legally able to raise Him from the dead and declared His Son to be righteous. Only an unrighteous man is subject to death. Therefore, God could raise Him from the dead.

Everything is going according to God's plan. Not only did Jesus fulfill the Law, but He will also fulfill all the prophecies concerning Him. Here is one prophecy concerning His triumphal entry into Jerusalem. Zechariah 9:9:

> 9 **Rejoice greatly, O daughter of Zion; shout, O daughter of Jerusalem: behold, <u>thy King cometh unto thee</u>: he is just, and having salvation; lowly, and <u>riding upon an ass,</u> <u>and upon a colt the foal of an ass.</u>**

Zion refers to Jerusalem, the City of God. Here, the prophet speaks about the arrival of Israel's King into Jerusalem. Matthew 21:5:

> 5 **Tell ye the daughter of Sion [Zion], <u>Behold, thy King cometh</u> unto thee, meek, and sitting upon an ass, and a colt the foal of an ass.**

Jesus fulfilled this prophecy when He entered Jerusalem days before He was crucified. Jesus Christ was their coming *King of Israel* was rejected by His own. John 1:10-11:

> 10 **He was in the world, and the world was made by him, and the world knew him not.** 11 **He came unto his own, and his own received him not.**

Notice the words of the throng of people who publicly declare Him to be the *Son of David*. Continue with Matthew 21:8-9:

> 8 **And a very great multitude spread their garments in the way; others cut down branches from the trees, and strawed them in the way.**

> 9 **And the multitudes that went before [Him], and that followed [after Him], cried, saying, <u>Hosanna to the Son of David</u>: Blessed is he that cometh in the name of the Lord; Hosanna in the highest.**

Later that day, Jesus was leaving Jerusalem with the disciples. They called His attention to the beauty of their Temple as the sun was setting. You may recall this from earlier. Can imagine the buildings appearing to be golden in the setting sun? However, Jesus shared with His disciples an ominous future. Read Matthew 24:2:

> 2 **And Jesus said unto them, See ye not all these things? verily I say unto you, There shall not be left here one stone upon another, that shall not be thrown down.**

Jesus was speaking about the future of Jerusalem. Forty has always been a significant number for God in the Bible. Usually, it denotes a period of testing. Think of Noah's forty days and forty nights, Israel's forty years in the Wilderness, and Jesus' forty days of testing. Jesus knew the destruction of Jerusalem and the Temple by Roman General Titus would occur in 70 A.D. That was exactly forty years after His crucifixion! Sitting alone with His disciples, they came and asked about the future. We continue with verses 3-4:

> 3 **And as he sat upon the mount of Olives, the disciples came unto him privately, saying, Tell us, when shall these things be? and what shall be the sign of thy coming, and of the end of the world?**

4 **And Jesus answered and said unto them, Take heed that no man deceive you.**

These are important questions: *When shall these things be? What shall be the sign of thy coming, and of the end of the world?* Jesus answers them. We must be careful to see this dispensationally. These apostles were Jews and they saw everything through the Law, the covenants, and the prophecies. There can be no question they are referring to the fulfillment of the Kingdom and His return as King.

We will look at Jesus' response. First, you need to know something. Jews came to expect miracles, signs, and wonders as a means of authentication of God's message. For them to be sure that it was God speaking or doing something, God had assured them the messenger would be authenticated. For that reason, Jesus did miracles. During the end times, the Antichrist and the Beast will produce counterfeit miracles, signs, and wonders. That is why Jesus told them to *Take heed that no man deceive you*. The words *take heed* means to *pay careful attention*. False prophets include preachers who misinterpret the Bible and deceive others. However, there is a standard by which everything can be compared. God will never do or say anything contrary to *The Word of God!*

The Twelve asked Him about the future concerning Israel and the Kingdom. He goes into some detail about what they will observe – miracles, signs, and wonders. He speaks of wars and rumors of wars. Then, He tells them, "see that ye be not troubled: for all these things must come to pass, but the end is not yet" (v.6). The entire chapter of Matthew 24 concerns the end times which will include famines, pestilences, and earthquakes. Let us look at verses 12-14:

12 **And because iniquity [sin] shall abound, the love of many shall wax [grow] cold.** 13 **But <u>he that shall endure unto the end, the same shall be saved</u>.**

14 **And this <u>gospel of the kingdom</u> shall be preached in all the world for a witness unto all nations; and then shall the end come.**

There are two important points above. Jesus said, "But he that shall endure unto the end, the same shall be saved" (v. 13). Remember this remark as it will be very important later. I will remind you again when it is appropriate. Also, Jesus specifically referred to "this Gospel of the Kingdom" (v. 14). We studied the promise of the eternal kingdom that God made to King David. We looked at Daniel's prophecy concerning the establishment of this kingdom.

Now, we read Jesus' words to His Twelve referring to the "Gospel of the Kingdom."

Let us answer the questions, "What caused the temporary suspension of the Age of Law?" Jesus taught the Jews, there was one sin that would not be forgiven them. Matthew 12:31-32:

> 31 **Wherefore I say unto you, All manner of sin and blasphemy shall be forgiven unto men: <u>but the blasphemy against the Holy Ghost shall not be forgiven</u> unto men.**
>
> 32 **And whosoever speaketh a word against the Son of man, it shall be forgiven him: <u>but whosoever speaketh against the Holy Ghost, it shall not be forgiven him, neither in this world, neither [nor] in the world to come.</u>**

Everything else will be forgiven, but blasphemy against the Holy Spirit would not.

Now, let us go to the book of Acts. Stephen was a righteous servant of God. Right now, I suggest you stop reading, grab your Bible, and read Acts chapters 6 and 7. Unfortunately. we do not have the space to include the entire story. It will greatly improve your understanding. Stephen had just stood before the rulers of Israel and charged them with grievous actions against God. He ends by accusing them of killing their Messiah. Their response is not unlike others who, when confronted with the truth, react explosively. As a result, the rulers of Israel had Stephen stoned to death as a blasphemer. Take heed as there is a lot going on here. Acts 7:54-57:

> 54 **When they heard these things, they were cut to the heart, and they gnashed on him with their teeth. 55 <u>But he [Stephen], being full of the Holy Ghost</u>, looked up stedfastly into heaven, and saw the glory of God, and Jesus standing on the right hand of God,**

> 56 **And said, Behold, I see the heavens opened, and the Son of man standing on the right hand of God. 57 Then they cried out with a loud voice, and stopped their ears, and ran upon him with one accord,**

Stephen, being *"filled with the Holy Spirit,"* was killed by stoning. The Sanhedrin is the highest court of justice and the supreme council of Israel. These rulers charged and executed Stephen as a "blasphemer" while he was visibly filled with the Holy Spirit. It was the rulers who committed blasphemy against the Holy Spirit. They did not listened to Jesus when he told them "blasphemy against the Holy Ghost shall not be forgiven" (Matt. 12:31). Stephen was a righteous man and filled with the Holy Spirit and they found him guilty of blasphemy!

There are some interesting words spoken by Stephen before he died. Gazing up to heaven, he said, "I see the heavens opened, and the Son of man standing on the right hand of God" (Acts 7:56). Jesus was seated at the right hand of God, but now He was standing. The rulers of Israel crucified their Messiah. Yet, God still endeavored to get the rulers to repent. He sent Stephen who, being filled with the Holy Spirit, spoke to them. Their hearts were hardened and they did not repent. They killed God's Son and the prophet He sent them. The destiny of this present evil generation was sealed! Verse 58:

> **58 And [they] cast him [Stephen] out of the city, and stoned him: and the witnesses [those doing the stoning] laid down their clothes at <u>a young man's feet, whose name was Saul</u>.**

Saul, who would later be known as Paul, appeared out of nowhere. The importance of his lack of association and familiarity with Jesus and His Twelve will become important later. At this point, a dispensational change is occurring. We must pay attention or, like most Christians, we will miss it completely.

We see the narrative change. Luke, the writer of Acts, began to follow this man, Saul. Acts 9 is a great chapter. It forms the first dispensational division in the New Testament. Most Christians are familiar with Paul's conversion on the Road to Damascus. He made it his mission to round up these Jewish apostates who were now following the Kingdom Gospel. His intention was to bring them back to Jerusalem to be judged by the same council that judged Stephen. Acts 9:1-2:

> 1 **And Saul, yet breathing out threatenings and slaughter against the disciples of the Lord, went unto the high priest,**
>
> 2 **And desired of him letters to Damascus to the synagogues, that if he found any of this way, whether they were men or women, he might bring them bound unto Jerusalem.**

Saul undergoes a life-changing confrontation with the Risen Savior in verses 3-5:

3 And as he journeyed, he came near Damascus: and suddenly there shined round about him a light from heaven:

4 And he fell to the earth, and heard a voice saying unto him, Saul, Saul, why persecutest thou me?

5 And he said, Who art thou, Lord? And the Lord said, I am Jesus whom thou persecutest: it is hard for thee to kick against the pricks.

A "prick" is "a stick, usually with a pointed end, used to poke or prod cattle to get them to move." Now, God had Saul's attention. See what the Lord tells him to do. Verses 6-9:

6 And he [Saul] trembling and astonished said, Lord, what wilt thou have me to do? And the Lord said unto him, Arise, and go into the city, and it shall be told thee what thou must do.

7 And the men which journeyed with him stood speechless, hearing a voice, but seeing no man.

8 And Saul arose from the earth; and when his eyes were opened, he saw no man: but they led him by the hand, and brought him into Damascus.

9 And he was three days without sight, and neither did eat nor drink.

Once Saul had settled into Damascus, God directed a man named Ananias to go to him. Saul was well-known to the Kingdom Believers and they feared him. Verses 10-14:

10 And there was a certain disciple at Damascus, named Ananias; and to him said the Lord in a vision, Ananias. And he said, Behold, I am here, Lord.

11 And the Lord said unto him, Arise, and go into the street which is called Straight, and enquire in the house of Judas for one called Saul, of Tarsus: for, behold, he prayeth, 12 And hath seen in a vision a man named Ananias coming in, and putting his hand on him, that he might receive his sight.

13 Then Ananias answered, Lord, I have heard by many of this man, how much

evil he hath done to thy saints at Jerusalem: 14 And here he hath authority from the chief priests to bind all that call on thy name.

Saul's reputation had preceded him. God discloses to Ananias what His plans were for him. Pay close attention to why God chose Saul. Verses 15-18:

15 But the Lord said unto him [Ananias], Go thy way: <u>for he [Saul] is a chosen vessel unto me, to bear my name before the Gentiles, and kings, and the children of Israel</u>:

16 For I will shew him how great things he must suffer for my name's sake. 17 And Ananias went his way, and entered into the house; and putting his hands on him said, Brother Saul, the Lord, even Jesus, that appeared unto thee in the way as thou camest [here], hath sent me, that thou mightest receive thy sight, and be filled with the Holy Ghost.

18 And immediately there fell from his eyes as it had been scales: and he received sight forthwith, and arose, and was baptized.

Whoa, Dobbin! To whom was God sending Saul to bring His message? Now, this is important. Until this point in Scripture, the gospel message was to be brought only to the Jews. Remember, Jesus commanded the Twelve saying, "Go not into the way of the Gentiles, and into any city of the Samaritans enter ye not: But [instead] go rather to the lost sheep of the house of Israel" (Matt 10:5-6). Did you notice, that Saul will be carrying his message to the Gentiles? That is quite a change. You may have a lot of questions, but be cautious. We must never apply our own assumptions! It is critical that we let the *Word of God* speak to us directly. He is the only trustworthy Source for our answers.

Most followers of Covenant Theology believe that Christ is currently King and ruling from heaven. There are three problems with this view. First, David's kingdom is earthly and not heavenly. Jerusalem, the City of God, will be its capital. God promised an heir to the Davidic dynasty Who would be an eternal king and sit on David's earthly throne. Consider Psalm 110:1:

> 1 **The LORD said unto my Lord,**
> **Sit thou at my right hand, until**
> **I make thine enemies thy footstool.**

Here, the LORD, Elohim, is speaking to David's Lord, Adonai, Who is Jesus Christ. Second, there is currently a *god of this world* who has not yet been defeated. (See 2 Cor. 4:4.) Third, in Daniel's prophecy, God states He will fulfill six items when His Kingdom is established on earth. They are to: (1) finish transgression, which is sin, (2) make an end of sin completely, (3) make a reconciliation for iniquity, which is a payment in full for sin, (4) bring in everlasting righteousness, (5) seal up, or fulfill, the prophecies, and (6) anoint the Most Holy – Jesus Christ the King. None of these have occurred yet! Additionally, the seven last years of Daniel's prophecy still remain to be completed.

We have reached a stopping point. We are looking at two theological paths. One is well trod upon and the other is not. This reminds me of my favorite poem by Robert Frost. Here are the last lines: "Two roads diverged in a wood, and I—I took the one less traveled by, and that has made all the difference." As we continue, we will take the path "less traveled by" and, I assure you dear Theophilus, that will make all the difference!

Follower of the *Word of God*,
Dr. David Alan Greene

Chapter 10

To Theophilus:

If we asked most Christians to tell us how many apostles there were, most will confidently state that there were twelve. For that reason, I call the Apostle Paul "the other apostle" and we will find out that this is a true statement. I was a student at a Christian College and asked my pastor at the Methodist Episcopal church, why he never preached from Paul's books. He told me that it is because Paul persecuted the church. Therefore, his seminary chose to ignore his teaching. They may find, should they ever choose to look, the following biblical evidence to be quite surprising.

The Age of Grace

We are taking the path less traveled by and, with good reason, you may never have heard this before. I will show you when the next dispensation began. It is called the *Age of Grace* and it is unlike its predecessors. Why? This current age or dispensation neither replaces nor runs concurrent with its former. Instead, it temporarily suspended the *Age of Law*. That is correct. The *Age of Law* was placed in abeyance. It was stopped and will resume when the present age ends. Like a stopwatch or the time countdown on a scoreboard, the remaining time is held until it resumes. Daniel's prophetic timeline was temporarily stopped after 483 years. This suspending occurred when two things happened. First, the Messiah was "cut off." Second, the rulers of Israel committed the unpardonable sin. The Countdown Clock for Daniel's prophecy shows seven years remaining.

Truth is never popular. I have staked my professional reputation on this. However, do not take my word for it! You need to see the biblical evidence and am here to show you. What happened when the *Age of Law* was suspended is one side of the dispensational change. The other side has to do with what happened to initiate the new dispensation we call the *Age of Grace*. Do you remember the circumstances under which we met Saul? The dispensational change centers around him! The narrative changes in the book of Acts as God appoints Saul who becomes the Apostle Paul.

We will see that the first convert during the *Age of Grace* was the Apostle Paul. Therefore, the *Age of Grace* begins with his conversion. There are different ways for me to approach this. I have chosen to allow the Bible to speak. Do you remember what God told Ananias? He said that Paul would be His "chosen vessel" for a specific purpose. What was that purpose? We read in Acts 9:15:

> **15 But the Lord said unto him [Ananias], Go thy way: <u>for he [Paul] is a chosen vessel unto me, to bear my name before the Gentiles, and kings, and the children of Israel</u>:**

Paul did preach in the synagogues of the Jews after his conversion. He continued to reason with them from Scripture that Jesus was the Messiah. The remainder of Acts follows the ministry of Paul to the Gentiles. Truth is never popular. He was fought tooth and nail along the way by the religious establishment. There is a lot of power, control, and money in established religion.

Immediately after the book of Acts, the thirteen Pauline epistles follow for good reason. Notice the transition at the end of the book of Acts. In the closing verses of Acts 28, the Apostle Paul made a formal declaration to Israel. Luke records this for us in Acts 28:28-29:

> 28 **Be it known therefore unto you, that the salvation of God is sent unto the Gentiles, and that they will hear it.**

> 29 **And when he had said these words, the Jews departed, and had great reasoning among themselves.**

So, at the close of Acts, we find Paul was done arguing with the Jews. He focused on the Gentiles because they would hear it.

At this point, we are going to examine some of Paul's letters. There is one in which he wrote to the Galatians in which he provides them with some historical events. We will examine them and their significance. Paul's affiliation with the other apostles was nonexistent. Later, it was limited to only a few meetings. During the persecution, the Twelve remained in Jerusalem. The following verse has Paul returning to Jerusalem. Note his lack of familiarity with the others. Galatians 2:1:

> 1 **Then fourteen years after I went up again to Jerusalem with Barnabas, and took Titus with me also.**

114

Paul met with the other apostles in Jerusalem so would know his message and the instructions he received from the Risen Savior. Verse 2:

> 2 **And I went up by revelation, and communicated unto them <u>that gospel which I preach among the Gentiles</u>, but privately to them which were of reputation, lest by any means I should run, or had run, in vain.**

Paul brought Barnabas and Titus with him. It becomes apparent from the text that Paul had not personally met the Twelve. He was unaware of those who were in charge. Verses 3-5:

> 3 **But neither Titus, who was with me, being a Greek, was compelled to be circumcised:**
>
> 4 **And that because of false brethren unawares brought in, who came in privily to spy out our liberty which we have in Christ Jesus, that they might bring us into bondage: 5 To whom we gave place by subjection, no, not for an hour; that the truth of the gospel might continue with you.**

In this epistle, Paul wrote to Gentile believers in Galatia. He explained the details of this private meeting. He makes a reference to *false brethren unawares brought in*. He never yielded to objections so that *the truth of the gospel might continue with you*, Galatians. These are curious statements. However, they made sense to the Galatians and soon they will make sense to you. We are about to get to the heart of the matter.

This meeting continued. Verses 6-7:

6 But of these who seemed to be somewhat, (whatsoever they were, it maketh no matter to me: God accepteth no man's person:) for they who seemed to be somewhat in conference added nothing to me:

7 But contrariwise [on the other hand], when they saw that the gospel of the uncircumcision [Gentiles] was committed unto me, as the gospel of the circumcision [Jews] was unto Peter;

Most likely you have never seen or heard any of this information before. People may despise Paul because he persecuted the Church. However, God place him in the Bible with thirteen epistles for a good reason. The above was so important, Paul repeated it in verse 8:

8 (For he that wrought effectually in Peter to the apostleship of the circumcision, the same was mighty in me toward the Gentiles:)

The *Uncircumcision* represents those who are the beneficiaries of the Abrahamic Covenant. It is another name for the Children of Israel. On the other hand, the *Uncircumcision* refers to those outside that covenant – the Gentiles.

In the next verse, Paul referred to James, Peter, and John as those *who seemed to be pillars* or the ones in authority. Verse 9:

9 And when James, Cephas, and John, who seemed to be pillars, perceived the grace that was given unto me, they gave to me and Barnabas the right hands of fellowship [they came to an agreement]; that we [Paul and Barnabas] should go unto the heathen [Gentiles], and they [the Twelve should go] unto the circumcision [Jews].

Pay particular attention to their response. They extended the *right hand of fellowship.* This signified that

They had accepted his position. They were in agreement. Can you see a clear division here? Each of these two parties would carry their unique gospel to two distinctly different recipients: the Jews and Gentiles respectively. Going forward, you need to see there are two different gospels. The Twelve would take their gospel to the Circumcision or Jews. Paul will take his gospel to the Gentiles called the Uncircumcision.

The word *gospel* comes from the Greek word *euanggelion* which means *good news*. The *Kingdom Gospel* is good news for the Jews. It is about the fulfillment of the promises God made to their fathers. The good news for the Gentile is known as the *Gospel of Grace!* These statements are like the opening arguments in a trial. They present what the attorneys believe to be the truth. Then, evidence is presented to support their position. We will provide evidence to support these statements as we continue. It took me two years of looking for additional evidence before I was totally convinced. So, take your own time and look to the Holy Spirit as your guide. When you read a verse, use the dispensational *tool*. See it within the context of who wrote it and to whom it was written. You can gain your interpretation dispensationally.

118

Your mind is probably flooded with questions. You may never have heard this information presented before. It may be difficult for you to reconcile this with everything you have been taught. We talked about this at the beginning. I said, "With crisis comes resolution." Pray about it and wait for God to answer your questions. It is natural to have questions. At the moment, we must leave some of them unanswered until later. There is much more evidence to consider before making a premature decision.

We will set aside Paul's Gospel of Grace as we now focus on the Kingdom Gospel. We need to see what comprises the Gospel of the Kingdom. This is the gospel message preached to the *Uncircumcision*. It is the same message preached by Jesus and the Twelve. Notice to whom Jesus sent His disciples. He gave them careful instructions. Matthew 10:5-6:

> 5 **These twelve Jesus sent forth, and commanded them, saying, <u>Go not into the way of the Gentiles</u>, and into any city of the Samaritans enter ye not: 6 <u>But go rather to the lost sheep of the house of Israel</u>.**

The recipients are clearly stated. They to go to the lost sheep of Israel. What was the gospel message that Jesus proclaimed? These following verses from the Gospels will clarify His gospel's message:

Mark 1:14-15:

> 14 Now after that John was put in prison, Jesus came into Galilee, preaching the gospel of the kingdom of God, 15 And saying, The time is fulfilled, and the kingdom of God is at hand: repent ye, and believe the gospel.

Matthew 4:23:

> 23 And Jesus went about all Galilee, teaching in their synagogues, and preaching the gospel of the kingdom, and healing all manner of sickness and all manner of disease among the people.

Matthew 9:35:

> 35 And Jesus went about all the cities and villages, teaching in their synagogues, and preaching the gospel of the kingdom, and healing every sickness and every disease among the people.

In Matthew chapter 24, Jesus spoke specifically about the end times. Verse 14:

14 And <u>this gospel of the kingdom</u> shall be preached in all the world for a witness unto all nations; <u>and then shall the end come.</u>

This verse refers to the final seven years. Therefore, during the Tribulation and until the end, this message of the Gospel of the Kingdom will be preached. It will be preached by the two prophets and the 144000 witnesses. We will discuss this later.

The Gospel of the Kingdom concerns the fulfillment of the kingdom promised to King David. Jeremiah 31:31-34:

31 Behold, the days come, saith the LORD, that <u>I will make a new covenant with the house of Israel, and with the house of Judah</u>:

32 Not according to the covenant that I made with their fathers in the day that I took them by the hand to bring them out of the land of Egypt; which my covenant they brake, although I was an husband unto them, saith the LORD:

33 But <u>this shall be the covenant that I will make with the house of Israel</u>; After those days, saith the LORD, <u>I will put my law in their inward parts, and write it in their hearts; and will be their God and they shall be my people</u>.

34 And they shall teach no more every man his neighbour, and every man his brother, saying, Know the LORD: for <u>they shall all know me, from the least of them unto the greatest of them</u>, saith the LORD: for <u>I will forgive their iniquity, and I will remember their sin no more</u>.

Notice that Israel sins will be forgiven when their Messiah returns and the eternal Kingdom is established. God is faithful and will not change. What God has promised, He will accomplish. Faith is the act of believing what God said. Believing the *Word of God!*

In the next letter, we will look at the *Gospel of Grace* and compare it with the *Gospel of the Kingdom*.

Loving the *Word of God*,
Dr. David Alan Greene

Chapter 11

To Theophilus:

We will define Paul's *Gospel of Grace* and compare it to the *Gospel of the Kingdom*. Before we do this, it is important for me to remind you of the origin of *Dispensational Theology*. It came from the Apostle Paul. He knew that the two gospels must be seen separately. Their messages were different. The recipients of these messages were different. Therefore, a clear division must be seen in order for them to stand separately. By dividing the Bible, the two gospels make sense and their recipients easily seen.

Paul was imprisoned in Rome. He knew his death was imminent. Here, he wrote his last letter to Timothy with these instructions. It is these instruction we now use to correctly interpret the *Word of God*. 2 Timothy 2:15:

15 [Timothy,] Study to shew thyself approved unto God, a workman that needeth not to be ashamed, [by] <u>rightly dividing the word of truth</u>.

In his last words to Timothy, Paul told him to apply this approach to the *Word of God*. It is this same *tool* of "carefully cutting" or "rightly dividing" that we are now applying. Scripture has not changed, but our method of observation has.

Allow me to tell a story as an example of rightly dividing. When I spoke at my doctoral graduation service, I brought a box of large brass paperclips. (With an adult present, you may want to try this at home.) The ushers gave each person one of these paperclips. I held up a paperclip and stated it is a wonderful example to help people to understand their Bible. As I looked out over the congregation, I could see most of them thought I was joking. The brass paperclip was tied to the theme of my dissertation and provided an illustration of rightly dividing *The Word of God*.

I directed them to locate the pages in their Bible beginning with Romans and ending with Philemon. I asked them to paperclip these pages together. They had successfully divided the New Testament into three divisions: the front, the middle, and the back.

124

Since I was in an evangelical church, I knew I was addressing only Gentiles. I told them the entire Bible is written *for us.* The Bible as a whole gives us knowledge and understanding of God. However, these books paperclipped in the center of the New Testament were different. They were the letters written by Paul who was called the Apostle to the Gentiles. As Gentiles, these pages held inside the paperclip were written *to us!*

As I explained to them, I am now explaining to you. The first division of the New Testament comprises the Matthew, Mark, Luke, John, and Acts. The Gospels are historical narratives of the Messiah's earthly ministry to the Jews. Acts records the transition from the Jews to the Gentiles. Do you remember Paul's proclamation? Acts 28:28:

28 Be it known therefore unto you, that the salvation of God is sent unto the Gentiles, and that they will hear it.

Before we examine Paul's epistles, held within the paperclip, let us summarize the division of the New Testament that follows Paul's epistles. These books, beginning with Hebrews and ending with Revelation, are written to the Jews. These are often referred to as the Hebrew epistles. With the exception on Hebrews, all of them were written to the Jews by one of the Twelve. According to the agreement made in Galatians 2, this group would continue to preach and teach the *Kingdom Gospel* to the *Circumcision*.

The *Age of Grace* caused a temporary suspension of *Age of Law*. It is often referred to as a *parenthetical interruption*. Like a comment placed within parentheses in a sentence (like this example), it does not affect the sentence itself. The sentence continues unaffected after the *parenthetical interruption*. When the *Age of Grace* ends, the Age of Law resumes unaffected. The stopwatch continues with the remaining seven years. These Hebrew epistles and the book of Revelation were written to the Jews. Why? Remember what Jesus told his disciples. Matthew 24:13:

> 13 **But he that shall endure unto the end, the same shall be saved.**

They have no choice but to go through the Tribulation in order to receive their salvation.

Now, with that said, we can focus on Paul's unique message. We learned that God chose Paul to be His chosen vessel. Acts 9:15:

> 15 **But the Lord said unto him [Ananias], Go thy way: <u>for he [Paul] is a chosen vessel unto me, to bear my name before</u>**

the Gentiles, and kings, and the children of Israel:

Paul was the human vessel God chose to carry His message to the Gentiles. He would also carry it to kings and the children of Israel were also welcome to listen and respond as well. This message received by Paul had never been revealed before. For that reason, Paul referred to it as a *mystery*. The word *mystery* means something that is *unknown*. Let us verify that this was indeed a *mystery* until God revealed it to Paul. Romans 16:25:

> 25 **Now to him that is of power to stablish you according to my gospel, and the preaching of Jesus Christ, according to the revelation of the mystery, which was kept secret since the world began,**

In another verse, we see that this revelation of the mystery was given to Paul. Colossians 1:25-27:

> 25 **Whereof I am made a minister, according to the dispensation of God which is given to me for you, to fulfil the word of God;**
>
> 26 **Even [that is to say] the mystery which hath been hid from ages and from**

generations, but now is made [known] manifest to his saints:

27 To whom God would make known what is the riches of the glory of this mystery among the Gentiles; which is Christ in you, the hope of glory:

When you read in the KJV and see the word "even" try replacing that word with the phrase "that is to say." The words that follow either expound upon or reemphasize what was already said. If we do this, then verse 26 would mean "that is to say the mystery which hath been hid from ages and from generations, but now is made known to his saints." Saints are those who choose to believe the gospel after hearing it preached. Here are some more verses that supports this: Romans 12:3, 15:15, 1 Corinthians 3:10, 2 Corinthians 13:10, Galatians 2:9, and Ephesians 3:2, 3:7. I am sure you will enjoy finding other golden nuggets on your own.

So, why Paul? He spoke of his sinful past as one who persecuted Christ. He called himself the *chief* of sinners. Yet God, in His mercy, saved Paul by His grace. The pastor who told me that his seminary did not teach Paul because he persecuted the church should read this! God chose Paul for that very reason. He was to be a *pattern,* a prototype; an example.

If he could be saved by God's grace, then anyone could! 1 Timothy 1:12-13:

> **12 And I thank Christ Jesus our Lord, who hath enabled me, for that he counted me faithful, putting me into the ministry; 13 [I, Paul] Who was before a blasphemer, and a persecutor, and injurious: but I obtained mercy, because I did it ignorantly in unbelief.**

Paul was to carry the same gospel message that saved him. The same work that Christ did in him, he would proclaim to the Gentiles. Verses 14-15:

> **14 And the grace of our Lord was exceeding abundant with faith and love which is in Christ Jesus.**

> **15 This is a faithful saying, and worthy of all acceptation, that <u>Christ Jesus came into the world to save sinners; of whom I am chief [the worst]</u>.**

Why would God do such a thing? The answer is found in verse 16:

> **16 Howbeit for this [reason] cause I obtained mercy, that in me [as the] first**

Jesus Christ might shew forth all long-suffering, <u>for a pattern</u> [an example] <u>to them which should hereafter believe on him to life everlasting</u>.

The word translated as *pattern* in the Greek is *deiknumi*. This means *to reveal something physically*. Paul was to be a pattern for other sinners who would hear the message and believe by faith. Those saved by grace through faith are to follow Paul's example. He is an incredible example for other sinners. God's grace is sufficient for everyone and that includes the worst of sinners!

How did Paul receive this revelation? He explained this in Galatians 1:11-12:

11 But I certify you, brethren, that the gospel which was preached [by] of me is not after man.

12 For I neither received it [from] of man, neither was I taught it [by man], <u>but by the revelation of Jesus Christ</u>.

He made it clear that the gospel he preached was not received from men such as the other apostles. The two gospels were never mingled. He made it clear Who gave him this gospel message. It was the Lord

Jesus Christ who revealed this *good news* to him.

Paul proved that this privilege was not bestowed upon him in recognition of anything worthy he had done. In fact, it was quite to the contrary. He did not earn this. It was given to him as a gift. Verses 13-14:

> 13 **For ye have heard of my conversation [life actions] in time past in the Jews' religion, how that beyond measure I persecuted the church of God, and wasted it:**
>
> 14 **And profited [advanced] in the Jews' religion above many my equals in mine own nation, being more exceedingly zealous of the traditions of my fathers.**

Paul's actions did not deserve this. He certainly did not earn salvation. Yet, Christ revealed this *mystery* to Paul and no one else. Verses 15-17:

> 15 **But when <u>it pleased God</u>, who separated me from my mother's womb, and called me by his grace, 16 <u>To reveal his Son in me</u>, that I might preach him among the heathen; immediately I conferred not with flesh and blood:**

17 Neither went I up to Jerusalem to them which were apostles before me; but I went into Arabia, and returned again unto Damascus.

Paul did not go to Jerusalem to consult with the other apostles. He went to Arabia. It appears from the following verses he was there for three years where he remained separated from the other apostles. It was not until many years later that he met with only Peter and James in Jerusalem.

Paul finishes his account of the facts like someone completing a legal affidavit. He testifies that his statements are true. Verses 18-20:

18 Then after three years I went up to Jerusalem to see Peter, and abode with him fifteen days. 19 But other of the apostles saw I none, save [except] James the Lord's brother. 20 Now the things which I write unto you, behold, before God, I lie not.

There are many ways to present the Bible. This approach has been to present the general framework. Then, we add specific verses to confirm what is being presented. These verses are to confirm the framework. Only true students of the Bible would be willing to take the time to do this. It is their love of the *Word of God* above all else. I fear that many readers have long put this book down because it conflicts with what they have been taught. For us, we must press on to finish outlining the framework. You should be getting excited. The end times will soon come into view.

This is how far we have come. We learned from Galatians 2, there are two separate gospels. One of them is the *Gospel of the Kingdom* and the other the *Gospel of Grace*. The Twelve remained committed to caring for the existing Kingdom Believers – the children of Israel and some proselytes. Paul remained committed to bringing his gospel to the Gentiles without excluding the Jews. These two gospels are different. We will continue and the comparisons will be made shortly.

God always deals with Israel as a group. They are a family – the children of Abraham. Their salvation will also be applied to them as a group. We learned that those who follow the Kingdom must endure until the end to receive their salvation. Jesus said, "But he that shall endure unto the end, the same shall be saved" (Matt. 24:13). This is true for the *Gospel of the Kingdom*, but it is completely different from Paul's *Gospel of Grace*.

Now, let us look at Paul's *Gospel of Grace* and compare the doctrinal differences with the *Gospel of the Kingdom*. There is a place where we can find Paul's gospel concisely stated. He wrote to the assembly of Grace Believers in Corinth. In his letter, he summarized the Gospel of Grace. Paul's letters were shared amongst the assemblies. What he wrote for one assembly was applicable for all and it still applies today. I have enumerated the parts of the gospel in the last verse. 1 Corinthian 15:1-4:

> 1 **Moreover, brethren, I declare unto you <u>the gospel</u> which I preached unto you, which also ye have received, and wherein ye stand; 2 <u>By which also ye are saved</u>, if ye keep in memory what I preached unto you, unless ye have believed in vain.**

> 3 **For I delivered unto you first of all that which I also received, <u>how that [1] Christ died for our sins according to the scriptures; 4 And that [2] he was buried, and that [3] he rose again the third day according to the scriptures:</u>**

Many have said, "Hold on a minute! Is that it? It sounds too simple! Why don't more people believe it?" That is the stumbling block. It is too simple!

Most evangelists find there are very few people who want to hear the truth. Do you remember the examples of Flood and the Promised Land? If we compare the simplicity of the Gospel of Grace with what is being taught in most churches today, then it most certainly sounds too simple. In fact, many learned men have said that it almost sounds foolish! Here is how Paul responded. 1 Corinthian in 1:18-20:

> 18 **For the preaching of the cross is to them that perish <u>foolishness</u>; but unto us which are saved it is the power of God.**
>
> 19 **For it is written, I will destroy the wisdom of the wise, and will bring to nothing the understanding of the prudent.**
>
> 20 **Where is the wise? where is the scribe? where is the disputer of this world? <u>hath not God made foolish the wisdom of this world?</u>**

It sounds like we should be careful of the learned or, should I say, professionals who make this simple gospel more complicated. Perhaps they, in their wisdom, should take heed! Paul continues with verses 21-25:

21 For after that in the wisdom of God the world by wisdom knew not God, it pleased God by the foolishness of preaching to save them that believe.

22 For the Jews require a sign, and the Greeks [Gentiles] seek after wisdom:
23 But we preach Christ crucified, unto the Jews a stumblingblock, and unto the [Gentiles] Greeks foolishness;

24 But unto them which are called, both Jews and Greeks, Christ the power of God, and the wisdom of God. 25 Because the foolishness of God is wiser than men; and the weakness of God is stronger than men.

We will show additional evidence that the only requirement for salvation under Paul's *Gospel of Grace* is faith. Here *faith* means *believing what God said*. This is what we found earlier with Abraham when he believed God, God counted to towards him as righteousness. Genesis 15:6:

6 And [Abraham] he believed in the LORD; and he counted it to him for righteousness.

It is all about believing the *Word of God*. This is what is called "saving faith." It is for this reason that Paul wrote, "it pleased God by the foolishness of preaching to save them that believe" (1 Cor. 1:21). With the *Gospel of Grace*, salvation is received the moment the person believes! This is the singular difference between the two gospels.

Let us take a look at Paul's letter to Grace Believers in Ephesus. 2:8-9:

8 For by grace are ye saved through faith; and that not of yourselves: it is the gift of God: 9 Not of works, lest any man should boast.

Here is an explained statement of the *Gospel of Grace*. It is still simple, but it shows how it becomes effective. Salvation is obtained (1) by *grace* (2) through *faith*. Notice that works is specifically excluded. *Grace* is a *gift*. *Faith* is *believing what God said*. The concept of *works* deals with the expectation of receiving payment for doing something. So, in other words, God offers salvation as a *gift*. It is free to anyone who believes. However, His gift can only be received by those who *believe His Word*. Works have no part in obtaining salvation. There is nothing we need to do, buy, provide, or make an exchange of value. The gift was paid in full by the death, burial, and resurrection of God's Son. We receive it *by faith.*

Today, many people struggle with this concept as they did in Paul's time. Here is how Paul responded to them. Romans 11:6:

> 6 **And if by grace, then is it no more of [by] works: otherwise grace is no more grace. But if it be of [by] works, then is it no more [by] grace: otherwise work is no more work.**

It is pretty simple. It must be one or the other. Either salvation is given as a gift or it is earned through working for it. It cannot be both. Then, it would be payment for our completed work.

Wages are earned. They are payment in exchange for work done. Paul compares the gift of grace offered by God with what we have actually earned. What we have earned for our sinful works is death. Romans 6:23:

> 23 **For <u>the wages of sin is death;</u> but <u>the gift of God is eternal life</u> through Jesus Christ our Lord.**

The *Gospel of Grace* offers salvation as a gift to anyone whether they are a Gentile or a Jew. It is free to all who will receive His gift by faith. What have we earned? As fallen sinners, we have earned death since the wages or penalty of sin. However, the gift of God through the *Word of God* is eternal life!

Here is a good time for another story. I taught a Bible class for seniors in a rural Baptist church. One of the attendees was delighted to finally see the Bible making sense. She was in her seventies and attended this church her whole life. Spending her winters in Florida, she approached her southern pastor excited about her Bible. Since she had learned to rightly dividing, it was now making sense. He told her he had never heard of such a thing and told her it would be best for her to stay away from it. And, that was it.

In the next letter, we will continue comparing the *Gospel of Grace* with the *Gospel of the Kingdom*.

Leaning on the *Word of God,*
Dr. David Alan Greene

Chapter 12

To Theophilus:

The Apostle Paul wrote, "When I was a child, I spake as a child . . ." (2 Cor. 13:11). I am going to allow my inner child to speak for a moment. As a child I might say that there are a "gazillion" objections when people hear how simple the *Gospel of Grace* is. I wondered why everyone cannot see it. It is so simple. Here is Paul's response. 2 Corinthians 4:3-4:

> **3 But if our gospel be hid, it is hid to them that are lost: 4 In whom the god of this world hath blinded the minds of them which believe not, lest the light of the glorious gospel of Christ, who is the image of God, should shine unto them**

Often Paul would present the gospel and stay with the new believers. Sometimes would stay for years as he taught them. A devout group of Jews would enter into these assemblies after Paul left. Many of them were Pharisees. They refuted Paul's gospel saying that the Law must be *included* in order to receive salvation. His gospel to the Gentiles was just too simple as there can be no status in achieving salvation as a gift. Many modern-day preachers, like the Pharisees, feel they must add something to this simple gospel.

As humans, we rationalize or reason. We learn what others teach and then teach it to others. This is exactly what happened to the Galatians. Paul writes to them concerning this. Adding or changing the Gospel of Grace makes it invalid! Galatians 1:6-7:

> 6 **I marvel that ye are so soon removed from him that called you into the grace of Christ unto another gospel:**
>
> 7 **Which is not another; but there be some [that believe to the contrary] that trouble you, and would pervert [change] the gospel of Christ.**

Some had come into their assembly and taught that the Law must be added to grace. Verses 8-9:

> 8 **But though we, or an angel from heaven, preach any other gospel unto you than that which we have preached unto you, let him be accursed.**

142

9 As we said before, so say I now again, <u>If any man preach any other gospel</u> unto you than that ye have received, <u>let him be accursed</u>.

This was so important that Paul repeated it! He said that anyone who changes the message which he preached to them will be cursed. So, don't be tempted to change Paul's *Gospel of Grace* in any way. Paul's gospel was all about Christ: His death, burial, and resurrection. None of it is about us! This upsets a lot of pious Christians who have worked so hard to get ahead of the others. I will stop there.

Here is another story. I was teaching a weekly Bible study at night to blue-collar men. When I finished explaining the *Gospel of Grace*, I thought one guy was going to explode. His face got all red. He abruptly stood up, his chair fell backwards, and he said, "What about *faith without works is dead!?!*" The room was completely silent. I thought, keep calm and carry on. I replied, "OK, let's take a look at those verses." As I looked up the verses, the others sat there. I found the verses and read them aloud from James 2:14-17:

14 What doth it profit [benefit], my brethren, though a man say <u>he hath</u>

faith, and have not works? can faith save him?

15 If a brother or sister be naked, and destitute of daily food, 16 And one of you say unto them, Depart in peace, be ye warmed and filled; notwithstanding ye give them not those things which are needful to the body; what doth it profit?

17 **Even so faith, if it hath not works, is dead, being alone.**

I asked, "Are these the verses you are talking about?" I was new at this and inside I was rattled since I had never before encountered such hostility. I like questions because it shows me someone is thinking. I continued, "OK, let's turn to the beginning of James and read the first verse." "Why!?!," he demanded. I told him I would read the verse and then I wanted to ask him a question. He agreed.

Since the group sat there listening to this, I read aloud James 1:1:

1 James, a servant of God and of the Lord Jesus Christ, to the twelve tribes which are scattered abroad, greeting.

He asked, "So, what's your question?" To which, I responded, "Which of the twelve tribes are you from?" There were twelve men in a small classroom and you could hear a pin drop. I am sure that not one of them forgot the lesson. When reading the Bible, we must know *dispensationally* where we are. It makes a huge difference! The book of James is part of the Hebrew epistles. The Apostle James wrote to the *Circumcision*. They are the Kingdom Believers who are still under the Mosaic Law. They follow the *Gospel of the Kingdom*. Paul wrote his epistles to the Gentiles. They follow the *Gospel of Grace*. This was a real-life case study. That night, they learned we cannot mix Grace with Law.

The *Age of Grace* is the reason for the temporary suspension of God's dealings with the Jews. They still have seven years on the clock. The current *Age of Grace* began with Paul's conversion. Christ gave Paul the *Gospel of Grace* to bring to the Gentiles. Today, many people follow instructions of the clergy by repenting and being baptized. Others are told to give their lives to Christ or make Him Lord over their life. This is called a *quid pro quo.* Lawyers use this Latin phrase which means *"something for something"* or *"this for that."* By doing this, there is an expectation that God owes them something. This is a common expectation given it is the way of the world. Paul gave this response. Romans 11:33-35:

> **33 O the depth of the riches both of the wisdom and knowledge of God! how unsearchable are his judgments, and his ways past finding out!**
>
> **34 For who hath known the mind of the Lord? or who hath been his counsellor?**
>
> **35 <u>Or who hath first given to him, and it shall be recompensed [repaid] unto him again?</u>**

God owes no one! What He is doing through grace is giving salvation to any who will believe the *Word of God*. Since no one can become righteous on their own, God did for us what needed to be done. Jesus Christ was born sinless. He lived a righteous life according to the Law. His death is sufficient for all, but only effective for those who choose to believe Him!

Compare this to the *Gospel of the Kingdom*. What does this gospel teach? We will look at Jesus' parting words given to His Apostles at His Ascension into heaven. Matthew 28:18-20:

18 **And Jesus came and spake unto them, saying, All power is given unto me in heaven and in earth.**

19 **Go ye therefore, and teach all nations, baptizing them in the name of the Father, and of the Son, and of the Holy Ghost:**

20 <u>**Teaching them to observe all things whatsoever I have commanded you**</u>**: and, lo, I am with you alway, even unto the end of the world. Amen.**

The is called the "Great Commission." Most, if not all, Christian churches follow these instructions today. However, these instructions were given to the apostles committed to the *Gospel of the Kingdom*. Remember His earlier commandment. Matthew 10:5-6:

5 **These twelve Jesus sent forth, and commanded them, saying, <u>Go not into the way of the Gentiles</u>, and into any city of the Samaritans enter ye not:**

6 <u>**But go rather to the lost sheep of the house of Israel.**</u>

The word *observe* means to keep His commandment by their actions. In other words, they must *do* what He taught them to *do.* The Jews who accept the *Kingdom Gospel* are *still* under the Mosaic Law. They are also saved by faith. However, they have a long history of losing their faith. So, God requires that their faith must be continual proven to be alive by their works. The verses we read in James confirm this. During the Tribulation, they are still under the Law. For them, nothing has changed! Paul's *Gospel of Grace* is different. Salvation is given as a gift, by God's grace, and received by faith. The key to understanding the Bible is seeing it dispensationally. It is important to remember that we cannot mix Grace with Law!

In the four gospels, we see Jesus and the Twelve preaching to the lost sheep of Israel exclusively. Yes, some Gentiles were saved. but they became proselytes of Israel. Jesus' ministry was "to confirm the promises made unto the fathers" (Rom. 15:8). There is a story of Greeks, another name for Gentiles, coming to speak with Jesus. He would not see them, but only responded to his disciples. John 12:20-24:

> 20 **And there were certain Greeks among them that came up to worship at the feast: 21 The same came therefore to**

Philip, which was of Bethsaida of Galilee, and desired him, saying, Sir, we would see Jesus.

22 Philip cometh and telleth Andrew: and again Andrew and Philip tell Jesus.

23 And Jesus answered them, saying, The hour is come, that the Son of man should be glorified. 24 Verily, verily, I say unto you, Except a corn of wheat fall into the ground and die, it abideth alone: but if it die, it bringeth forth much fruit.

Jesus gave no response to the Greeks. He only commented on His death which had future implications.

When we interpret the Bible dispensationally, the verses are meant to convey a message even if it is an allegory. Any message encompasses four parts: the sender, the message, the messenger, and the recipient. We must never force the interpretation of a verse into a particular system or, for that matter, ignore a verse since we cannot.

During His earthly ministry, Jesus taught using parables. The following one concerned Israel and the land promised to the fathers. Although Israel currently inhabits the land, it will be part of their inheritance when the Messiah comes and establishes His Kingdom. In the following parable, Jesus teaches about the owner of the land who left His vineyard in the care of husbandmen. These husbandmen, or caretakers, represent Israel. They occupied the land which God owns and He has given them the responsibility of managing it for Him. This owner sent multiple servants (prophets) over time to collect what was due Him. However, the caretakers killed these servants. Finally, we read in verses 37-38:

> 37 **But last of all he sent unto them his son, saying, They will reverence my son.**
>
> 38 **But when the husbandmen saw the son, they said among themselves, This is the heir; come, let us kill him, and let us seize on his inheritance.**

In this parable, the Son of this landowner was predicting His death at the hands of Israel. Also, notice, the inheritance belongs to the Son. If they killed the Son, then they could seize the land for themselves. Jesus told this parable for all to hear. These husbandmen or caretakers were the chief priests and Pharisees of Israel. This has special meaning for faithful Israel. Psalm 2:12:

12 Kiss the Son, lest he be angry, and ye perish from the way, when his wrath is kindled but a little. <u>Blessed are all they that put their trust in him.</u>

When we see this parable dispensationally, it makes sense. Providentially, God raised His Son from the dead. This same Son will receive His inheritance when His Kingdom is established.

The *Age of Grace* is a temporary suspension of the *Age of Law*. We identified that it began with Israel's rejection and Paul's conversion. But, when will the *Age of Grace* end? In the next letter, we continue to look at the *Age of Grace* and find its conclusion.

Faithful to the *Word of God,*
Dr. David Alan Greene

Chapter 13

To Theophilus:

In the previous chapter, we covered a lot of material. Think of it as describing individual pieces of a puzzle in great detail. We are fitting the pieces together. Gradually, we will see the full picture take shape. The more we continue, the greater the detail the picture will have. Only a few more dispensational pieces and we will be finished. We are approaching the end times chronologically. This may seem like a lot of work, but look how far we have come! The good news is we are on the sixth dispensation.

If we compare the *Gospel of Grace* and the *Gospel of the Kingdom*, then we see there is one major difference. The *Gospel of Grace* is not a covenant. It is an offer. As with most offers, there is an expiration date. After that date, it will no longer be possible to accept God's gracious offer of salvation by grace through faith alone. Those who deal with legal transactions might put it this way, "There is a current offer on the table. It will be withdrawn on the expiration date." Remember, we are answering the question, "When will the *Age of Grace* end?" One pastor told me that he did not want to be raptured. When I asked him why, he told me that he wanted to be left behind so that he could save more people. I thought about it. I asked him which gospel he would preach as the *Gospel of Grace* would no longer be available.

Some already understand how imminent the withdrawal of this offer is. For them, there is a sense of urgency to make this offer known to as many people as possible. At the Rapture, the offer expires. Like the day the door to the Ark was closed, so too will be the end of the *Age of Grace*. For those who rejected the offer, judgment is inevitable. Once that happens, the *Age of Law* will resume. The only message to be preached by the two witnesses and the 144000 is the *Gospel of the Kingdom*. How do we know that for sure. These are Jesus words. Matthew 24:14:

> 14 **And this gospel of the kingdom shall be preached in all the world for a witness unto all nations; and then shall the end come.**

Once the seven remaining years begin, they will be filled with much consternation. Those who remain

154

after the Rapture, there is no escape from the Tribulation.

Does the Bible tell us when the Rapture will happen? It does not give us an exact date. I believe God has His reasons. Paul does provide us with a "trigger" that will initiate the Rapture. This will bring the *Age of Grace* to its conclusion. In his letter to the Romans, he explains the purpose for the temporary suspension of the *Age of Law*. Towards the end, he makes the only comment concerning the end of this present age. Romans 11:25:

> **25 For I would not, brethren, that ye should be ignorant of this mystery, lest ye should be wise in your own conceits; that blindness in part is happened to Israel, <u>until the fulness of the Gentiles be come in.</u>**

The *mystery* of the Gospel of Grace was made known to Paul. He preached and taught it. Did you notice his comment on how long this temporary blindness would take place?

He said *until the fulness of the Gentiles be come in.* You might ask, "Well, how long is that?" It could refer to a specific number Gentiles or refer to a predetermined amount of time. It does not say. However, my personal belief is the latter. As we see from Daniel's prophecy, God works on a timetable that only He knows. What initiates the end is not specified, but we know there is a predetermined end. Once that occurs, the Lord will close the door to the *Age of Grace* like He closed the door to the Ark.

Writing to another assembly of Grace Believers, Paul used a reference to a timetable. He spoke of *the times and the seasons.* 1 Thessalonians 5:1-3:

> 1 **But of the times and the seasons, brethren, ye have no need that I write unto you.** 2 **For [you] yourselves know perfectly that <u>the day of the Lord</u> so cometh as a thief in the night.**

> 3 **For when they [the non-Believers] shall say, Peace and safety; then sudden destruction cometh upon them, as [unexpectedly as] travail [labor pains] upon a woman with child; and they [the non-Believers] shall not escape.**

Here, Paul addressed the suddenness of this occurrence. The Rapture marks the end of the *Age of Grace* and the resumption of the *Age of Law*. This will be the beginning of the Tribulation. The Tribulation is referred to as "the Day of the Lord" (v. 2).

156

The Day of the Lord is the dreaded time of God's testing and wrath. These verses are important for those wanting to know whether Grace Believers go through any part of the Tribulation. Look at what Paul wrote to Grace Believers. Verses 9-10:

9 For God hath not appointed us [Grace Believers] to wrath, but [rather] to obtain salvation by our Lord Jesus Christ,

10 Who died for us, that, whether we wake [alive] or sleep [physically dead], we should live together with him.

Here is an important fact to remember. Grace Believers cannot be appointed to wrath!!! Why not? It is because they received the righteousness of Christ when they believed. How can the righteousness of Christ be judged?

Here, the word *appointed* means *determined, fixed, or established by an order or command.* Look at verse 9 again. We will restate it using different words. Paul was speaking to those who were already saved by grace through faith. He said God did not appoint them to wrath. Wrath is punishing. Instead, He appointed them to obtain salvation *in Christ.* When they chose to believe the Gospel of Grace, they were placed *in Christ.* They were sealed by the Holy

Spirit like the occupants of the Ark. They obtained their salvation and it is secure by being placed in the Lord Jesus Christ.

With that said, we need to return to the use of the word *predestinated* from a previous verse. Paul does not teach that God determined the salvation of each individual's salvation in advance. However, God has predetermined something. We are going to look at three verses. The first is Romans 8:28:

> 28 **And we know that all things work to-gether for good to them that love God, <u>to them who are the called according to his purpose</u>.**

Do you remember when we previously discussed God's purpose? We read, "For this is good and acceptable in the sight of God our Savior, Who *will have all men to be saved and to come unto the knowledge of the truth*" (1 Tim. 2:3-4). The Sovereign God desires that all men should come to the saving knowledge of truth. It is part of His overall plan to restore Creation. Foreknowledge is part of God's ability to know everything in advance. God's omniscience is part of His character. However, to foreknow and to predetermine are two different actions. They are not the same. Verse 29:

29 **For whom he did foreknow, he also did predestinate to be conformed to the image of his Son, that he [Christ] might be the firstborn [first to be resurrected] among many brethren.**

God knew in advance those who, by their own free will, would choose to accept His gracious offer. Now, concerning them, He did predetermine something. What was that? He determined in advance that *they would be conformed to the image of His Son.* Is this something believers must do for themselves? No! Grace Believers are *in Christ.* They have *His righteousness.* They are co-heirs with Him. For them, God predetermined the results which He accomplished through His Son. There is nothing to be done. We must not be confused. God did not determine, in advance, who would and would not be saved.

The word *called* creates problems for some until it is explained. 2 Timothy 1: 9-10:

9 [God] Who hath saved us, and called us with an holy [separate] calling, not according to our works, but according to his own purpose and grace, <u>which was given [to] us in Christ Jesus before the world began,</u>

10 But is now made manifest by the appearing of our Saviour Jesus Christ, who hath abolished death, and hath brought life and immortality to light through [the preaching of] the gospel:

Grace Believers are saved by believing. They exercised their free will and chose to accept God's offer. It was the gift believers would receive that was predetermined before the world began. God offers this gift to everyone. However, it is only received when someone chooses to believe it! Here is another verse using the word *predestinated*. Ephesians 1:3-4:

3 Blessed be the God and Father of our Lord Jesus Christ, who hath blessed us with all spiritual blessings in heavenly places in Christ:

4 According as he hath chosen us [those who accept His offer of grace] in him [Christ] before the foundation of the world, that we [Grace Believers] should be holy [separate] and without blame [righteous] before him [God] in love:

Read these verses again in your own Bible. The bracketed words will help you when you read the original text.

160

As much as this may offend some, it is not about us. It is all about Christ! It was never about us earning salvation or God predetermining salvation of individuals in advance. It is about those who, by their own free will, choose to accept God's gift by faith. The result for those who do choose to accept was predetermined by God. Those who believe are placed securely *in Christ*. This not only explains the issue surrounding the word *predestinated*, but it also encapsulates the entire message of the *Gospel of Grace*. Let us finish Paul's thought. Verses 5-6:

5 Having predestinated us [Grace Believers] unto the adoption of children by Jesus Christ to himself, according to the good pleasure of his will,

6 To the praise of the glory of his grace, wherein <u>he hath made us accepted in the beloved.</u>

It was predetermined that, collectively, Grace Believers would be placed in Jesus Christ. That was God's purpose from the very beginning. Verses 7-9:

7 In whom we [Grace Believers] have redemption through his blood, the for-

giveness of sins, according to the riches of his grace;

8 Wherein he hath abounded toward us [Grace Believers] in all wisdom and prudence;

9 Having made known unto us the mystery of his will [Gospel of Grace], according to his good pleasure which he hath purposed in himself:

Let us summarize. If Grace Believers have the righteousness of Christ, as previously stated, then they cannot be judged. God declared Christ to be righteous. How can He judge those who are *in Christ?* To do that, God must show wrath or judgement towards His Own Son. In another letter to the same church, Paul repeated much of what we have seen before, but he adds a portion applicable to Grace Believers. 2 Thessalonians 2:1:

1 Now we beseech you, brethren, by <u>the coming of our Lord Jesus Christ</u>, and <u>by our gathering together unto him</u>,

This refers to His Appearing and not to His Second Coming. The Lord Jesus Christ will appear in the air to collect His purchased possession. He will do this before the coming wrath to come. Paul just described the Rapture. Here, the conjunction *and* the two happen simultaneously. Consider this example. The father showed up at the party and he brought ice cream. These words – *and by our gathering together unto Him* – make it clear this is the Rapture. The will gather to Himself all those who were purchased by His blood. They are called *the Body of Christ* and this event is called *The Blessed Hope*.

Paul wrote about this future event to encourage Grace Believers. With the impending judgement, he did not want them to be shaken in mind or spirit. Neither did he want them deceived. Verses 2-3:

> 2 **That ye be not soon shaken in mind, or be troubled, neither by spirit, nor by word, nor by [false] letter as [if] from us, as that the day of Christ is at hand.**

> 3 **Let no man deceive you by any means: for that day shall not come, except there come a falling away first, and that man of sin be revealed, [Antichrist] the son of perdition;**

Paul is explaining the details of the coming Tribulation. The appearance of the Antichrist is something

That Grace Believers will not see. Verse 4:

> **4 Who [Antichrist] opposeth and ex-
> alteth himself above all that is called
> God, or that is worshipped; so that he
> [Antichrist acts] as God sitteth in the
> temple of God, shewing himself [Anti-
> christ] that he is God.**

Then, Paul reminds them that he had told them this
in person. All of the following verses concern the Antichrist. Verses 5-6:

> **5 Remember ye not, that, when I was yet
> with you, I told you these things? And
> now ye know what withholdeth that he
> [Antichrist] might be revealed in his
> time.**

It is the Holy Spirit Who is holding back this evil. The
reason for this delay is *until the fulness of the Gentiles
be come in.* Once that happens, the Rapture will occur
and then the Antichrist will be revealed. The last
seven years of Daniel's prophecy will resume.

We previously discussed the word *mystery*. It
means *something not known or not yet revealed.* The
Gospel of Grace was a *mystery* until God revealed it
to Paul. There is a counterfeit of this. It is called the

164

mystery of iniquity. The man of evil whom no one has seen will now be revealed in the flesh . He is the Wicked One or Antichrist. Those who remain on earth after the Rapture will have the unique opportunity of seeing evil incarnate. Verses 7-12:

> 7 For the <u>mystery of iniquity</u> doth already work: only he who now letteth will let, until he be taken out of the way.
>
> 8 And then shall that Wicked [Antichrist] <u>be revealed,</u> whom the Lord shall consume with the spirit of his mouth, and shall destroy with the brightness of his coming:
>
> 9 Even him [Antichrist], whose coming is after the working of Satan with all power and signs and lying wonders, 10 And with all deceivableness of unrighteousness in them that perish; because they received not the love of the truth, that they might be saved. 11 And for this cause God shall send them <u>strong delusion,</u> that they should believe a lie: 12 That they all might be damned [1] who believed not the truth, [2] but had pleasure in unrighteousness.

A delusion is a false belief that is fixed in someone's mind. It is not open to change even in view of conflicting evidence to the contrary. Wait a minute! Paul wrote about the final days in his epistle. Have we seen any evidence of this happening? These words were written to Grace Believers to encourage and motivate them to share the *Gospel of Grace!*

Although the word *Rapture* is not specifically used in the Bible, it has come to describe *the Catching Away.* Grace Believers in Thessaloniki were concerned they had been left behind. They looked at all the persecution going on around them. They thought they had missed the Rapture and were living in the Tribulation. They were also concerned about the Grace Believers who had already died. What would happen to them? Paul addressed these issues in 1 Thessalonians 4:13-14:

> 13 **But I would not have you to be ignorant, brethren, concerning them which are asleep [already died], that ye sorrow not, even as [that is to say like] others which have no hope.**

> 14 **For if we believe that Jesus died and rose again, even [that is to say] so them also which sleep in Jesus will God bring with him.**

166

It is not an issue for Grace Believers whether they are dead or alive at the Rapture. Verse 15:

15 For this we say unto you by the word of the Lord, that we which are alive and remain unto the coming of the Lord shall not prevent [precede] them which are asleep.

Living believers will not go before those believers who sleep. All Grace Believers are spiritually alive *in Christ* from the moment of their salvation when they receive the Holy Spirit. Paul taught that it is the Holy Spirit Who guarantees the fulfillment of the promised redemption. More on that shortly.

Paul summarized the Rapture. Verses 16-17:

16 For the Lord himself shall descend from heaven with a shout, with the voice of the archangel, and with the trump of God: and the [physically] dead in Christ shall rise first:

17 Then we which are alive and remain shall be <u>caught up together with them in the clouds, to meet the Lord in the air</u>: and so shall we ever be with the Lord.

The Lord does not descend to earth. He remains in the air. Grace Believers who have died are still alive *in Christ.* They will be raised from the grave first. Immediately after that, Grace Believers who are still alive will join with them to meet the Lord in the air. From that point, they will never be separated from the Lord Jesus Christ.

The Rapture is called *The Blessed Hope* for a reason. This is evident as Paul ends with these words of encouragement. Verse 18:

> 18 **Wherefore comfort one another with these words.**

Paul repeated this theme in his letter to Titus. There he spoke of encouraging other believers, but also being zealous of doing good works. Not that the works earns or guarantees our salvation. These works are a natural outpouring of gratitude to One Who did it all for us. Titus 2:13-14

> 13 **Looking for that blessed hope, and the glorious appearing of the great God and our Saviour Jesus Christ;**
>
> 14 **Who gave himself for us, that he might redeem us from all iniquity, and**

purify unto himself a peculiar people, zealous of good works.

Looking for the *Blessed Hope,*
Dr. David Alan Greene

Chapter 14

_____

To Theophilus:

The main events of the Tribulation were highlighted in Daniel 9, Matthew 24, and some of Paul's writings. Here is a key point to remember. Those saved by grace through faith are gone! Following their Rapture, only two groups will remain: the Children of Israel and the Nations. Like in the Days of Babel, they will gather together for one singular purpose. Following the Antichrist, they will seek to annihilate God's people – Israel. God will never allow that to happen. He will return to defend Israel and avenge their enemies.

The Tribulation is divided into two equal halves. You will see three and one-half years, forty-two months, or 1260 days. They are the same thing. The last half is considered the Great Tribulation. Jesus spoke of this in Matthew 24:21-22:

21 For then shall be great tribulation, such as was not since the beginning of the world to this time, no, nor ever shall be.

22 And except those days should be shortened, there should no flesh be saved: but for the elect's sake those days shall be shortened.

The word *elect* refers to Israel. It is not the Body of Christ since they have been removed. Only the Jews and Gentiles remain. God chose or elected Abraham because of his faith. The Abrahamic Promise was not conditional. Therefore, God will fulfill the covenant. He will do this for the sake of His elect, the Children of Israel. God cut short the time of the Great Tribulation from all seven years to only three and one-half years.

We will start with the second half – the Great Tribulation – by going to Revelation 12. Much of Revelation is written allegorically. I am sure the Lord had His reasons. We will try to stay on course and focus on how the Tribulation fits into the overall biblical framework.

We find a woman who represents Israel. She is giving birth to a child. From the context, we can figure out the parties involved. Verses 12:3-5:

> 3 And there appeared another wonder in heaven; and behold a great red dragon, having seven heads and ten horns, and seven crowns upon his heads.

> 4 And his tail drew the third part of the stars of heaven, and did cast them to the earth: and the dragon stood before the woman which was ready to be delivered, for to devour her child as soon as it was born.

> 5 And she brought forth a man child, who was to rule all nations with a rod of iron: and her child was caught up unto God, and to his throne.

The great red dragon represents Satan and, at this point in time, he is extremely angry. The stars refer to angels. One third part of these angels Satan took with him when he rebelled against God. This dragon seeks to devour this child as soon as it is born. Herod's massacre of the innocents happened at the time when Christ was born. His evil intent was to kill the woman's *man-child*. Satan did not stop there as he purposed evil men to plot against this Child of God to crucify Him. That would end His plan to restore Creation. Notice what it says about this child. The man-child was (1) to rule all nations with a rod of iron and (2) was caught up unto God and to his throne. Following this death, God raised Him from the dead and seated Him a throne at His right hand.

The next verse confirms we are at the mid-point of the Tribulation. The woman represents Israel. Verses 6:

6 And the woman fled into the wilderness, where she hath a place prepared of God, that they should feed her there a thousand two hundred and threescore days.

There is that number I mentioned. It confirms that we are in the last half or 1260 days on the Great Tribulation. From Israel's beginning, Satan has attempted to destroy Israel represented here by the woman. The verse tells us that God will provide for Israel in much the same way as He did in the Wilderness.

The book of Revelation has details of all the judgements to come. The book of Revelation gets its name from the revelation of the Lord Jesus Christ.

Paul provided us with details on this in his letter to the Colossians. About Jesus Christ, he wrote in Colossians 1:15-18:

> 15 Who [Christ] is the image of the invisible God, the firstborn [first resurrected from the dead] of every creature: 16 For by him [Christ] were all things created, that are in heaven, and that are in earth, visible and invisible, whether they be thrones, or dominions, or principalities, or powers: all things were created by him [Christ], and for him [Christ]:
>
> 17 And he [Christ] is before all things, and by him [Christ] all things consist. 18 And he [Christ] is the head of the body, the church: who [Christ] is the beginning, the firstborn [first resurrected] from the dead; <u>that in all things he [Christ] might have the preeminence</u>.

The book of Revelation accomplishes two important goals. It records the completion of God's restoration of fallen Creation. It also records the revelation of the Lord Jesus Christ Who is God. These verses give a wonderful summary of Who Christ really is. In the end, Jesus Christ will be revealed to all Creation. Philippians 2:10-11:

10 That at the name of Jesus every knee should bow, of things <u>in heaven</u>, and things <u>in earth</u>, and things <u>under the earth</u>;

11 And that every tongue should confess that Jesus Christ is Lord, to the glory of God the Father.

Paul explained God's purpose for doing this in Colossians 1:19-20:

19 For it pleased the Father [God] that <u>in him</u> [Christ] should all fulness dwell;

20 And, having made peace [between God and Creation] through the blood of his cross, <u>by him</u> [Christ] to reconcile all things unto himself [God]; by him [Christ], I say, whether they be things in earth, or things in heaven.

Verses 20 is so important. By having the fullness of all things dwell in Christ, His death on the Cross was the singular event which made peace between *all things and God*. It accomplished everything, but it did so at a very high cost – the sacrifice of His Son.

In the Fall, both Mankind and Creation fell from God's grace. With the fullness of all things dwelling in Christ, His sacrifice allowed God to reconcile all things to Himself. This is not "universal salvation." Christ's death made it possible that all *can* be saved. Christ's death was *sufficient* to reconcile all things. However, it will only be *efficient* for those Who believe the *Word of God!*

Let us repeat God's sovereign plan for Mankind. 1 Timothy 2:4:

> 4 **Who [God] will have all men to be saved, and to come unto the knowledge of the truth.**

Everyone will not be saved even though this is God's desire. He will not force people to be saved but allow them to exercise their free will. God wants people to choose to love Him. They must make their own choice. Universal salvation for all Mankind is possible, if it were not for man's free will. He allows everyone to accept or reject His offer.

It is during the Tribulation that Christ's preeminence is being achieved. This includes the Body of Christ, Israel, and the Gentiles. Continue with verses 5-6:

5 For there is one God, and one mediator between God and men, the [same] man Christ Jesus;

6 Who gave himself [as] a ransom for all, to be testified [revealed] in due time.

All that He has done will be revealed to Creation in due time.

During the Tribulation, the Mosaic Covenant is, once again, in effect. It was a conditional covenant which includes what is called the *blessings and curses*. These are dependent upon the actions of Israel. If Israel keeps all the points of the Law, then God will bless them. However, if they break just one point of the Law, then God will curse or punish them. These blessings and curses are *earthly*. Israel's future, their Kingdom, and the Davidic throne are all earthly. The capital of the Kingdom will be Jerusalem which is a physical city on earth. So, the *Gospel of the Kingdom* and the *Gospel of Grace* are different! The former is earthly and the latter heavenly. Without a dispensational view of Scripture, this difference would be lost on most readers.

Let us consider this further by going back to the beginning of Genesis. It shows that God divided His Creation from the very beginning. Genesis 1:1:

1 In the beginning God created <u>the heaven and the earth</u>.

So, God began by dividing His Creation into two parts: *heaven* and *earth*.

In the Abrahamic Covenant, God promised that it will be Abraham's *Seed* who will receive the *Land* as an inheritance. Paul explained that this inheritance is not conditional. Galatians 3:16-17:

16 Now to Abraham and <u>his seed</u> were the promises made. He saith not, And to seeds, as of many; but as of one, And <u>to thy seed, which is Christ</u>.

17 And this I say, that the covenant, that was confirmed before of God in Christ, the law, which was four hundred and thirty years after, cannot disannul, that it should make the promise of none effect [worthless].

Many Jews will say that they receive this inheritance by keeping the Law. Paul refuted that in Galatians 3:18:

18 For <u>if the inheritance be of the law</u>, <u>it is no more of promise</u>: but God gave it to Abraham by promise.

God promised the land to Abraham. There were no strings attached. There were no conditions to meet in order to receive it. It was *unconditional.* The gift was given to Abraham and his Seed which is Christ – the Son of Abraham and Son of King David. Those who are true Israel are Jews who follow the *Gospel of the Kingdom.* To receive salvation, they must endure until the end.

Israel's inheritance under the Gospel of the Kingdom is earthly. If that is so, then what is the inheritance of those saved by the *Gospel of Grace?* We will look at verses from Ephesians. Paul wrote to those saved by grace. Being saved, Paul tells them there is so much more for them than their salvation. They have an *inheritance!* Ephesians 1:11-12:

11 In whom [Christ] also we have obtained an <u>inheritance</u>, being predestinated according to the purpose of him [God] who worketh all things after the counsel of his own will:

12 That we [being saved by His Grace] should be to <u>the praise of his glory</u>, who first trusted in Christ.

We already discussed the word *predestinated.* Our focus will now be on the *inheritance.* Continue with verses 13-14:

13 In whom [Christ] ye also trusted, after that <u>ye heard the [preaching of the] word of truth</u>, the gospel [message] of your salvation: in whom [Christ] also after that ye believed [by faith], ye were sealed with that holy Spirit of promise,

14 Which [Who] is <u>the earnest of our inheritance</u> until the redemption of the purchased possession, unto the praise of his glory.

For those saved by grace through faith, the Holy Spirit is immediately given to them. The word *earnest,* as used above, is a legal term. It means *a binding deposit made for the purpose of guarantying the fulfillment of a promise.*

That would be our *promised inheritance.* Now, let look at read Ephesians 1:18:

18 The eyes of your understanding being enlightened [by hearing the gospel of your salvation]; that ye may know what is the hope of his [Christ's] calling, and what the riches of the glory of his [Christ's] <u>inheritance</u> [which is] in the saints,

An *inheritance* is not something received now, but something will in due time. Furthermore, an *inheritance* is not something that is earned. It is a *gift* received by a legitimate heir. So, how are those who are saved by grace through faith considered to be an heir? Paul told us that it is Christ Who will receive the inheritance. Grace Believers, being *in Christ,* are co-heirs with Him. Romans 8:16-17:

> **16** The Spirit itself beareth witness with our spirit, that <u>we are the children of God</u>:
>
> **17** And <u>if children, then heirs; heirs of God, and joint-heirs with Christ;</u> if so be that we suffer with him [Christ], that we may be also glorified together [with Him]

Paul offers these words of praise to the One from Whom all these blessings flow. Ephesians 1:6:

6 To the praise of the glory of his [God's] grace, wherein he [God] hath made us accepted <u>in the beloved</u> [Christ].

God is working to reconcile His Creation to Himself. He will reconcile Israel to Himself when the Kingdom is established and their Messiah is proclaimed their King. During the *Age of Grace*, God reconciled Gentiles to Himself. Colossians 1:20:

20 And, having made peace through the blood of his cross, by him [Christ] <u>to reconcile all things</u> unto himself [God]; by him [Christ], I say, whether they be things in earth, or things in heaven.

Notice the words "to reconcile all things unto Himself." Do you remember the divisions God made at the Creation? See the words "whether they be things in earth or things in heaven."

There will be both Gentiles and Jews who reject God's gracious offers of reconciliation. In fact, they will opposed Him. The rebellious will be dealt with severely during these final years. The *Gospel of the Kingdom*, the same message that Jesus preached on earth, will be preached once again. They will proclaim the Kingdom of God is at hand! Repent!! However, like those who rejected Noah's pleadings to repent, they too will suffer the consequences of God rejecting God's offer.

Is the Tribulation necessary? Yes. God's is testing His people. Only true Israel who have faith in the *Word of God* will be saved, but only if they endure to the end. God is reconciling all things to Himself through His Son. Ephesians 1:10:

> 10 **That in <u>the dispensation of the fulness of times</u> he might <u>gather together in one all things in Christ, both which are in heaven, and which are on earth;</u> even [that is to say] in him:**

This verse is referring to a future dispensation which follows the Tribulation. It will happen and we can be confident it will. At the completion of the seven years, everything will be reconciled *in Christ*. This coming dispensation, called the *Dispensation of the Fulness of Time*, is the *Millennial Age* or the *Millennial Reign*. This new dispensation will happen after the Second Coming of Christ.

As we finish this chapter, I would like you to consider something. Traditional dispensational theology has seven dispensations like what we are presenting, but they have each following the other sequentially. This is a mistake. The *Age of Grace* is sandwiched between the *Age of Law*. Previously, I called it a "parenthetical interruption." The pattern looks like A-B-A where A is the *Age of Law* and B is the *Age of Grace*. We know that God created the heaven and earth in seven days. How many of the seven days did God work? The Bible answers this in Genesis 2:1-3:

> 1 **Thus the heavens and the earth were finished, and all the host of them. 2 <u>And on the seventh day God ended his work which he had made; and he rested on the seventh day from all his work which he had made.</u>**

> 3 **And <u>God blessed the seventh day, and sanctified it: because that in it he had rested from all his work which God created and made.</u>**

In the next chapter, we will continue with the *Dispensation of the Fulness of Time*. Everything is working according to God's plan. He will gather all things – both in heaven and on earth – *in Christ!*

Your brother *in Christ,*
Dr. David Alan Greene

Chapter 15

To Theophilus:

Here are a few words of encouragement for you. When we lived in New Hampshire, we would hike the White Mountains often. After a couple hours, it would get tougher the closer we got to the top. However, the views at the top made it worth it! We have only two dispensations of the seven left! Next up is the *Dispensation of the Fulness of Time* in which God finishes His work. When contractors get close to the end of a job, they have a punch list that includes everything they need to do to finish the job.

At the end of the seven last years, the Tribulation or Testing was complete. We have a list that God said He would fulfill given in Daniel's prophecy. I want to state them again here. Here is the list of six items:

(1) finish transgression, which is sin,
(2) make an end of sin completely,

(3) make a reconciliation for iniquity, which is payment in full for sin,

(4) bring in everlasting righteousness,

(5) seal up, or fulfill, the prophecies; finally,

(6) anoint the Most Holy.

In this chapter, we will look at what God has accompanied so far.

The Age of the Fulness of Time

The *Dispensation of the Fulness of Time* is also called the Millennial Age. You will see that its length of one thousand years is mentioned in the following text. Revelation 20:1-3:

> 1 **And I saw an angel come down from heaven, having the key of the bottomless pit and a great chain in his hand.**
>
> 2 **And he laid hold on the dragon, that old serpent, which is the Devil, and [also called] Satan, and bound him a thousand years,**
>
> 3 **And cast him into the bottomless pit, and shut him up, and set a seal upon him, that he should deceive the nations no more, till [until] the thousand years**

should be fulfilled: and after that he must be loosed [released] a little season.

This dispensation has to do with the *dispensing* of judgements. Satan will be judged first. He will be imprisoned for one thousand years to prevent him from deceiving the Nations.

Those who were faithful to Jesus Christ, the *Word of God,* and endured the Tribulation will be rewarded. Verse 4:

> 4 **And I saw thrones, and they sat upon them, and judgment was given unto them: and I saw the souls of them that were beheaded for the witness of Jesus, and for the word of God, and which had not worshipped the beast, neither his image, neither had received his mark upon their foreheads, or in their hands; and they lived and reigned with Christ a thousand years.**

The faithful who had been beheaded during the Tribulation because of their testimony to *The Word of God* include the 144,000 witnesses. They will reign with Christ for the *one thousand years.* They were resurrected because they endured unto death. This is the *first resurrection.* Verses 5-6:

5 But the rest of the dead lived not again until the <u>thousand years</u> were finished. This is the first resurrection.

6 Blessed and holy is he that hath part in the first resurrection: on such the second death hath no power, but they shall be priests of God and of Christ, and shall reign with him a <u>thousand years</u>.

From verse 6, we see that faithful Israel will be resurrected first. They were called to be the priests of God and of Christ. They too will reign with Christ for the thousand years. They were part of the first resurrection.

At the end of the one thousand years, Satan will be loosed for a short while. He will not have changed. In spite of the past history and the thousand-year reign of Christ, many have forgotten Satan's previous rebellion and defeat. Undeterred, Satan gathers many of the nations to make war against God and His people again. The size of their army is described as: *the number of whom is as the sand of the sea.* However, their moment of defiance against God is short lived. It ends with sudden and violent judgment from God. Revelation 20:7-9:

7 And when the <u>thousand years</u> are expired, <u>Satan shall be loosed out of his prison,</u>

8 And shall go out to <u>deceive the nations</u> which are in the four quarters of the earth, Gog and Magog, <u>to gather them together to battle</u>: the number of whom is as the sand of the sea.

9 And they went up on the breadth of the earth, and compassed the camp of the saints [God's people] about, and the beloved city [Jerusalem]: and fire came down from God out of heaven, and devoured them. [Wham!]

Satan, the instigator and leader of rebellions, will be punished for eternity. Verse 10:

10 And the devil that deceived them was cast into the lake of fire and brimstone, where the beast and the false prophet are, and shall be tormented day and night <u>for ever and ever.</u>

The following verses concern what is called the Great White Throne Judgement. This singular event is the final judgment. It leads to the Second Death which is described by the Apostle John who writes the details of this event as an eyewitness.

The scene that John describes is befitting for such a serious occasion. The earth and heaven flee from the face of Him Who is to pronounce this necessary judgement. All the dead, from all the ages past, will be summoned to rise again for their arraignment. As they stand before Him, the book of deeds and the book of life are opened. Verses 11-13:

> 11 **And I saw a great white throne, and him that sat on it, from whose face the earth and the heaven fled away; and there was found no place for them.**
>
> 12 **And I saw the dead, small and great, stand before God; and the books were opened: and another book was opened, which is the book of life: and the dead were judged out of those things which were written in the books, according to their works.**
>
> 13 **And the sea gave up the dead which were in it; and death and hell delivered up the dead which were in them: and they were judged every man according to their works.**

Judgement will be meted out based upon their works. Some sins are worse than others. Punishment will be determined based upon *those things which were written in the books, according to their works.*

Following this judgement, there are two items that are no longer needed in a righteous and restored Kingdom. That is death and hell. We read in verses 14-15:

> 14 **And death and hell were cast into the lake of fire. This is the second death.** 15 **And whosoever was not found written in the book of life was cast into the lake of fire.**

All this is part of the process in which God works to complete His purpose. Judgement will be part of the restoration of fallen Creation. This is necessary to establish the eternal Kingdom ruled by its worthy and righteous King.

Of the six items promised in Daniel's prophecy, there is one last item: the anointing of the Most Holy. We all know this will be Jesus Christ the Righteous One because no one else is worthy. He will be anointed to rule over the fully-restored Creation.

John described the new heaven and new earth in Revelation 21:1-2:

> 1 **And I saw a new heaven and a new earth: for the first heaven and the first earth were passed away; and there was no more sea.**
>
> 2 **And I John saw the holy city, new Jerusalem, coming down from God out of heaven, prepared as a bride adorned for her husband.**

All of us have seen a radiant bride as she walks down the aisle to meet her beloved. Verses 3-4:

> 3 **And I heard a great voice out of heaven saying, Behold, the tabernacle of God is with men, and he will dwell with them, and they shall be his people, and God himself shall be with them, and be their God.**
>
> 4 **And God shall wipe away all tears from their eyes; and there shall be no more death, neither sorrow, nor crying, neither shall there be any more pain: for the former things are passed away.**

Everything will be new! There will be no more sorrow, tears, death, crying, or pain. No longer will it exist because sin, its cause, has been irradicated. It would be difficult, if not impossible, to experience those things living in the presence of the Righteous King – the Creator of the Universe.

John continues with his description of the King in verses 5-6:

> **5 And he [Christ] that sat upon the throne said, Behold, I make all things new. And he [Christ] said unto me [John], Write: for these words are true and faithful.**
>
> **6 And he [Christ] said unto me [John], It is done [complete]. I am Alpha and Omega, the beginning and the end. I will give unto him that is athirst [thirsty] of the fountain of the water of life [to drink] freely.**

Christ speaks directly to those who overcame in verse 7. There is no doubt that He is speaking to true Israel who endured to the end. (See Matt. 24:13; Mk. 13:13.) Those who did not overcome will already have received their punishment. Verses 7-8:

7 <u>He that overcometh</u> shall inherit all things; and <u>I will be his God</u>, and <u>he shall be my son.</u>

8 But the fearful, and unbelieving, and the abominable, and murderers, and whoremongers, and sorcerers, and idolaters, and all liars, shall [continue to] have <u>their part in the lake which burneth with fire and brimstone: which is the second death.</u>

The judgements are completed prior to the arrival of the Bride in all her radiance – the New Jerusalem.

John mentions a particular angel, or messenger, by referring to his previous assignment. This same angel invites John to come and see the Bride of the Lamb. It is the New Jerusalem which is beautifully described by John in great detail. Count the memorials to Israel's history and the tribes of Israel in verses 9-21:

9 And there came unto me one of the seven angels which had the seven vials full of the seven last plagues, and talked with me, saying, Come hither [here], I will shew thee the bride, the Lamb's wife.

10 And he carried me away in the spirit to a great and high mountain, and shewed me that great city, the holy Jerusalem, descending out of heaven from God, 11 Having the glory of God: and her light was like unto a stone most precious, even like a jasper stone, clear as crystal;

12 And had a wall great and high, and had twelve gates, and at the gates twelve angels, and names written thereon, which are <u>the names of the twelve tribes of the children of Israel</u>:

13 On the east three gates; on the north three gates; on the south three gates; and on the west three gates. 14 <u>And the wall of the city had twelve foundations, and in them the names of the twelve apostles of the Lamb.</u>

15 And he that talked with me had a golden reed to measure the city, and the gates thereof, and the wall thereof. 16 And the city lieth foursquare, and the length is as large as the breadth: and he measured the city with the reed, twelve

thousand furlongs. The length and the breadth and the height of it are equal.

17 And he measured the wall thereof, an hundred and forty and four cubits, according to the measure of a man, that is, of the angel. 18 And the building of the wall of it was of jasper: and the city was pure gold, like unto clear glass.

19 And the foundations of the wall of the city were garnished with all manner of precious stones. The first foundation was jasper; the second, sapphire; the third, a chalcedony; the fourth, an emerald; 20 The fifth, sardonyx; the sixth, sardius; the seventh, chrysolite; the eighth, beryl; the ninth, a topaz; the tenth, a chrysoprasus; the eleventh, a jacinth; the twelfth, an amethyst.

21 And the twelve gates were twelve pearls; every several [separate] gate was of one pearl: and the street of the city was pure gold, as it were transparent glass.

The Apostle Paul's name is not included or mentioned as he has nothing to do with this earthly Kingdom. He is in heavenly places with the other saints saved by grace through faith.

The word *tabernacle* can be a noun which means *a meeting place*, or a verb which means *to dwell with*. In the case of Israel, this has great significance. The tabernacle constructed by their forefathers in the Wilderness was both a temporary meeting place and dwelling of God. Now, God intends to dwell with His people – Israel – forever. Notice the references to the Lamb as we continue with Revelation 21:22-23:

> **22 And I saw no temple therein: for the Lord God Almighty and the Lamb are [Themselves] the temple of it.**
>
> **23 And the city had no need of the sun, neither of the moon, to shine in it: for the glory of God did lighten it, and the Lamb is the light thereof.**

There are still the Gentile nations. They will bring their *glory and honor* which is their praise and offering to God. Verses 24-25:

> **24 And the nations of them which are saved shall walk in the light of it: and the kings of the earth do bring their glory and honour into it.**

25 And the gates of it shall not be shut at all by day: for there shall be no night there.

The nation of Israel was created by God for a peculiar or unique purpose. God spoke to Israel through Moses concerning this in Exodus 19:5-6:

5 Now therefore, if ye [Israel] will obey my voice indeed, and keep my covenant, then ye [Israel] shall be <u>a peculiar treasure unto me</u> above all people: for all the earth is mine:

6 And ye [Israel] <u>shall be unto me a kingdom of priests</u>, and <u>an holy nation</u>. [Moses,] <u>These are the words which thou shalt speak unto the children of Israel</u>.

The purpose of priests is to act as intermediaries between God and someone else. Who would this someone else be? Zechariah was a prophet in the 6th century B.C. over six hundred years before the birth of Christ. He wrote these words in Zechariah 8:20-23:

20 Thus saith the LORD of hosts; It shall yet come to pass, that there shall come

people, and the inhabitants of many cit-
ies:

21 And the inhabitants of one city shall
go to another, saying, Let us go speedily
to pray before the LORD, and to seek
the LORD of hosts: I will go also.

22 Yea, <u>many people and strong nations
shall come to seek the LORD of hosts in
Jerusalem,</u> and to pray before the
LORD.

23 Thus saith the LORD of hosts;
In those days it shall come to pass, that
ten men shall take hold out of all languages of the nations, even [they] <u>shall
take hold of the skirt</u> [hem of the gar-
ment] <u>of him that is a Jew, saying, We
will go with you: for we have heard that
God is with you.</u>

The Gentiles will know that the Jews have a
special relationship with God. Their unique purpose
will be to approach God on behalf of these other nations. They will be intermediaries for them. In the
new Creation, Christ will be with God and dwell in
the New Jerusalem. The *Nations* will go to Him and,

to do so, they can only approach Him through His priests – the nation of Israel.

Let us return to Revelation 21. Speaking of nations, kings, and the eternal city of Jerusalem, we read in verses 26-27:

26 **And they [the nations and the kings of the earth] shall bring the glory and honour of the nations into it [the eternal city].**

27 **And there shall in no wise [way] enter into it any thing that defileth, neither whatsoever worketh abomination, or maketh a lie: but they which are written in the Lamb's book of life.**

John continues to inspire our imagination as he describes the eternal City of God.

I hope you have been enjoying this as much as I have. In the next letter, we will continue with chapter 22 and bring the book of Revelation to its conclusion.

Trusting the *Word of God,*
Dr. David Alan Greene

Chapter 16

To Theophilus:

It is important to tie the concept of seven days of Creation with the seven dispensations of restoration. You might think, "Well hold on. If Adam sinned in the first dispensation, the *Age of Innocence*, then we can't count the first dispensation as part of the restoration." True, but I am referring to the restoration of another calamity.

This subject goes beyond the scope of this book. However, it does explain why God began His restoration with the *Age of Innocence*. There was a great calamity that preceded Adam. Otherwise, God would not have instructed Adam and Eve to "Be fruitful, and multiply, and replenish the earth" (Gen. 1:28). It is this catastrophe which resulted from the Great Rebellion that God is restoring His Creation. In the first dispensation of His restoration, God made Adam the caretaker or steward over His Creation. Genesis 2:15:

15 And the LORD God took the man, and put him into the garden of Eden to dress it and to keep it.

From the very beginning, Satan sought to derail God's plan for restoration.

The Bible provides two accounts of creation in Genesis. (See Genesis 1:1-2:3; 2:4-25.) The original creation of the world was completed in seven days. After the great calamity, God hovered or brooded over the deep surveying the total destruction. His restoration began when He recreated the world in which God made Adam. Again, He took seven days. In both records, God completed His work and rested on the seventh day. Here are some verses:

Genesis 2:3

3 And <u>God blessed the seventh day, and sanctified it: because that in it he had rested from all his work which God created and made</u>.

Exodus 20:11

11 <u>For in six days the LORD made heaven and earth</u>, the sea, and all that in them is, <u>and rested the seventh day</u>:

204

wherefore the LORD blessed the sabbath day, and hallowed it.

Hebrews 4:9-10

> 9 **There remaineth therefore a rest to the people of God.** 10 <u>**For he that is entered into his rest, he also hath ceased from his own works, as God did from his.**</u>

We are arriving at the accomplishment of God's ultimate purpose. It is called the Eternal Sabbath, Eternity, or Eternal Rest.

Revelation 22 is the last chapter and completes the New Testament. You may find it interesting that this chapter ties back to the very beginning of the Bible. We see the direct connection to the Garden of Eden. Revelation 22:1:

> 1 **And he shewed me a pure river of water of life, clear as crystal, proceeding out of the throne of God and of the Lamb.**

You may remember the declaration John the Baptist made when he saw Jesus approaching him. We read it in John 1:29:

29 The next day John [the Baptist] seeth Jesus coming unto him, and saith, <u>Behold the Lamb of God, which taketh away the sin of the world.</u>

Think about this. In which dispensation did John the Baptist say this? This was said during the *Age of Law* that he called Jesus Christ the Lamb of God, the Passover Lamb. In Revelation, the title *the Lamb* is a direct reference to the Passover Lamb and used eight times. Each time it refers to Jesus Christ.

This river flowing from *the throne of God and of the Lamb* is found in the middle of the street like a river enveloping an island. Here, we find the Tree of Life. In Genesis 3, God drove Adam and Eve from the Garden of Eden to prevent them from eating of the Tree of Life. Now that Creation has been restored, we find this same tree planted in the center of the New Jerusalem. Verses 2-5:

2 In the midst of the street of it, and on either side of the river, was there the tree of life, which bare twelve manner [types] of fruits, and yielded her fruit every month: and the leaves of the tree were for the healing of the nations.

3 And there shall be no more curse: but the throne of God and of the Lamb shall be in it; and his servants shall serve him:

4 And they shall see his face; and his name shall be in their foreheads.

5 And there shall be no night there; and they need no candle, neither light of the sun; for the Lord God giveth them light: and they shall reign for ever and ever.

The *Tree of Life* is once again found on earth! It will be located in the center of the New Jerusalem. God now provides the Light. From here, God and the Lamb together will reign forever and ever. The last item remaining on Daniel's checklist is the anointing of the Most Holy. That has now been completed.

God tells the Apostle John everything which was told to him is true. These events will happen. Revelation is about prophecy and the revealing of Jesus Christ. He tells John that those who keep or hold in their heart the truths of this book are blessed. Verses 6-7:

6 And he said unto me, These sayings are faithful and true: and the Lord God of the holy prophets sent his angel to shew unto his servants the things which must shortly be done.

7 Behold, I come quickly: blessed is he that keepeth the sayings of the prophecy of this book.

All of this had overwhelmed John and he fell at the angel's feet. He began to worship him, but the angel stopped him and reminded him that only God is worthy of praise. Verses 8-9:

8 And I John saw these things, and heard them. And when I had heard and seen, I fell down to worship before the feet of the angel which shewed me these things.

9 Then saith he [the angel] unto me, See thou do it not: for I am thy fellowservant, and of thy brethren the prophets, and of them which keep the sayings of this book: worship God.

The angel is a fellow servant of the Most High. He told John that what he learned should not be hidden. Since these events are imminent, he should make them known especially to his brethren. Notice what he says about allowing people to continue to be as they are. In other words, do not try to change them. As a prophet, he can only make known what God has revealed to him. Let people be as they are because there is little time left. John's vision occurred in the late first century prior to his death in 90 A.D. Verses 10-11:

> 10 **And he saith unto me, Seal not [Do not hide] the sayings of the prophecy of this book: for the time is at hand.**

> 11 **He that is unjust, let him be unjust still: and he which is filthy, let him be filthy still: and he that is righteous, let him be righteous still: and he that is holy, let him be holy still.**

The *Age of Law* is the dispensation about which John wrote. For the Jews, it is all about the earthly Kingdom and the Coming of their King Who will rule over the earth. The future is about Israel and the Gentile nations who will surround the earthly Kingdom.

It is a King's prerogative or right to reward those whom He chooses. There are those in the Kingdom who will receive rewards according to their works. The King says that these rewards are His alone to give. Verses 12-13:

12 And, behold, I come quickly; and <u>my reward is with me, to give every man according as his work shall be.</u>

13 I am Alpha and Omega, the beginning and the end, the first and the last.

Again, these are Kingdom Believers. Grace Believers have already received their reward and are in heaven. Blessed are they who are obedient to God. They will have access to the Tree of Life and be able to freely enter the enteral city, the New Jerusalem. Verses 14-15:

14 Blessed are they that do his commandments [follow His Laws], that they may have right to the tree of life, and may enter in through the gates into the city.

15 For without [outside] are dogs, and sorcerers, and whoremongers, and murderers, and idolaters, and whosoever loveth and maketh a lie.

Jesus makes a declaration to the Apostle John stating He is the rightful heir to the throne of David, King of Israel. It is important for the Jews to hear this. For Jesus Christ, the Creator, is calling Himself the

Root, meaning father, of King David. As Mary's son, He is also the Son of David. Therefore, He is both the root and the offspring of King David! Verse 16:

> 16 **I Jesus have sent mine angel [messenger] to testify unto you these things in the churches. I am <u>the root and the offspring of David</u>, and the bright and morning star.**

Before we read the next few verses, I would like to give you some history. In Paul's writings, he used the following allegory which can be applied to these verses in Revelation. They relate to the Bride of Christ. Galatians 4:22-23:

> 22 **For it is written, that Abraham had two sons, [Ishmael] the one by a bondmaid, [Isaac] the other by a freewoman.**
>
> 23 **But he who was of the bondwoman was born after the flesh; but he of the freewoman was by promise.**

You may recall from Genesis that Hagar, or Agar, was Sarah's handmaid. We find this story in Genesis. Sarah was unable to produce a child to fulfill God's promise to Abraham. Lacking in faith, she took matters into her own hands and had her husband sleep with her maid to obtain an heir. Hagar conceived a son through Abraham whose name was Ishmael. Then, according to the promise, God fulfilled the promise of an heir. He caused Sarah to conceive a child when she was very old. His name was Isaac. Paul spoke about two covenants: the Mosaic Covenant and the Abrahamic Covenant. With that, let us continue with verses 24-26:

> 24 **Which things are <u>an allegory: for these are the two covenants</u>; the one from the mount Sinai, which gendereth to <u>bondage</u>, which is Agar.**

> 25 **For this Agar is mount Sinai in Arabia, and answereth to Jerusalem which now is [present Jerusalem], and is in bondage with her children.**

> 26 **But Jerusalem which is above is <u>free</u> [the New Jerusalem], which is the mother of us all.**

The New Jerusalem from above is free. Again, God will fulfill His *promises!* These were unconditional *promises* made to Abraham and David. For this reason, the New Jerusalem, from above, is the Bride of Christ. Now, let us return to Revelation 22 and read verse 17:

17 **And the Spirit and the bride say, Come. And let him that heareth say, Come. And let him that is athirst come. And whosoever will, let him take the water of life freely.**

Revelation completes God's Word to mankind. It ends with a stern warning to anyone who alters the *Word of God.* A curse is placed upon anyone who adds words to or removes words from this book. God's revelation to Mankind was complete when John recorded what he saw and heard. Verses 18-19:

18 **For I testify unto every man that heareth the words of the prophecy of this book, If any man shall add unto these things, God shall add unto him the plagues that are written in this book:**

19 **And if any man shall take away from the words of the book of this prophecy, God shall take away his part out of the book of life, and out of the holy city, and from the things which are written in this book.**

The Apostle John ended the book by quoting the *Word of God* in verse 20:

20 He [Christ] which testifieth these things saith, Surely I [Christ] come quickly. Amen. Even so, come, Lord Jesus.

John blessed those who read the book in verse 21:

21 The grace of our Lord Jesus Christ be with you all. Amen.

If Daniel's calculations are correct, and I believe they are, then the 2000th anniversary of Christ's crucifixion will be in 2030 A.D. John was urged to proclaim the news he had received. Perhaps, we too should sense the urgency of the little time remaining . . . especially in this *Age of Grace.*

Proclaiming the *Word of God,*
Dr. David Alan Greene

Chapter 17

To Theophilus:

This is my last letter to you in this series. I hope you have gained an appreciation of rightly dividing the *Word of Truth*. Viewing the Bible *dispensationally* becomes a valuable tool. Many look at the biblical text up close without standing back. There is an old idiom: *Some cannot see the forest for the trees*. It describes people who are so close to the trees that they cannot see the forest or bigger picture. There are many who know an impressive amount of Scriptures, yet they struggle to make sense of it.

Is what Paul said true? Can we really be saved by grace through faith without works? Or, should we believe James who stated that faith without works is dead? Some rationalize that the latter verse applies after they have salvation. In other words, they receive their salvation as a gift, but to keep their salvation, they must do good works as proof of their faith.

Such a conundrum! However, when we look at the Bible *dispensationally,* we see the *Word of God* from God's perspective. Conflicts dissolve and, in their place, confidence appears. We know our salvation is secure and our position is *in Christ.* Remember, the *test of truth* must always be used when it comes to the validity of any interpretation.

I have one last story for you. Previously, I made references to putting pieces together and seeing the bigger picture. At the men's Bible study, I used an example to teach them an important lesson they would not forget. I bought three separate 1000-piece puzzles. These puzzles had one thing in common. The Bible? No, the focal point of each picture was a red barn. I broke all the pieces up and mixed all 3000 pieces into one big straw basket. In the class, I passed this basket around telling them to each take twenty-five pieces and place them face up on the table in front of them. They were free to look at each other's pieces so I gave them some time to discuss them. Then, I said, "Tell me about the picture." They could not say anything other than they thought whatever the focal point of the picture was red. They could not have a very clear picture, could they?

This symbolizes our own difficulties. Each puzzle box represented a different *system* of theol-

216

ogy: existential, convent, or dispensational. They were only able to look at what they had gleaned by choosing random pieces. This is the situation most Christians find themselves in. They have heard so many different teachers and preachers of the Bible. They have listened to podcasts and read popular books. They see only the *specifics,* but they have not seen the whole picture. You have!

After a while, I asked if it would help them if I showed them the pictures on the boxes. What? Pictures?!? Their shared response was groaning. Looking at the picture on the box gave them with a *general* perspective. It allowed them to see the "big picture" of the Bible. Then, it is easy to put together the smaller pieces correctly. This was one lesson they would always remember and I hope you can understand why.

Remember, truth is never popular. You may feel as though you are standing alone. To find others who are learning to rightly divide the *Word of Truth,* you should find a local assembly that teaches the Gospel of Grace. As of this printing, there is a web page that lists local assemblies. That list is maintained at: gracechurches.wordpress.com. I am not affiliated with the owner of the website. However, many of the assemblies listed have good reputations. Regardless of where you go, you are the one responsible for applying the *test of truth*.

The book *Letters to Theophilus* was specifically designed to be an introduction. Its purpose was to provide an overall framework of the Bible. Because of this purpose, many details of these individual dispensations were not included. Consider this book as directions on how to build a bookcase or framework for *dispensational theology*. Now, you can take your time, enjoy learning the details, and correctly place what you learn within their respective dispensations.

Here is another suggestion. If you have not read Genesis completely, start there. It records four of the seven dispensations! It is easy to understand because it used a narrative or story approach. Next, you should read Exodus completely. That book explains the beginning of the fifth dispensation – the *Age of Law*. This specifically applies to the Jews both then and after the Rapture. The *Age of Law* continues throughout the four Gospels. It is temporarily suspended in the latter half of the book of Acts. Remember, Jesus came to fulfill the promises God made to the fathers – Abraham, Isaac, and Jacob.

In the book of Acts, the first part of Acts recorded the beginning of the Kingdom Church. Pentecost is a Jewish celebration that comes fifty days after the Passover. It celebrates the firstfruits of the Jewish harvest. How appropriate! These new believers were committed to the *Kingdom Gospel*. This is the same gospel preached by Christ, and, later, by the Twelve. They agree with Paul, at the meeting in Galatians 2, to carry the *Kingdom Gospel* exclusively to the *Circumcision*. These Kingdom Believers must endure until the end to be saved. They must continually prove their faith by their works. The Great Commission was given to the Eleven. At His Ascension, they were told by Christ to teach the Kingdom Believers "to observe all things whatsoever I have commanded you" (Matt. 28:20).

The *Gospel of the Kingdom* remained the focal point until Stephen, the first martyr. (See Acts 6 and 7.) The transition to another dispensation began with Israel's official rejection by its rulers with the stoning of Stephen. At that point, we were introduced to Saul whose name later became Paul. In Acts 9, we read about Paul's conversion. God tells Ananias that he is His "*chosen vessel.*" Paul was the first person saved by the Gospel of Grace and for good reason. Since he was the worst of the worst sinner, he became the pat tern or prototype by which all others who are saved by grace should follow.

Do you remember how we separated Paul's letters or epistles using a large paperclip? For this current *Age of Grace*, they are *the* singular most important part of the Bible. Go ahead and paperclip them together if you have not done so. It will remind you of this! At first, it may feel challenging to read Paul's letters. There is the Grace Bible Commentary series listed in the back of this book. These commentaries take you verse-by-verse through the Bible applying right division. They are easy to read and, like these letters, offer explanations as you read the biblical text.

Theophilus, one who loves God, I have enjoyed writing you these letters. It has been a journey from Genesis to Revelation. If you have questions, you can always use the Contact Us form on the publisher's website.

I would like to close by sharing some words of encouragement from a letter I received from Jon and Susan McMahon. They are my beloved brother and sister in Christ and fellow Grace Believers. I keep their letter in my Bible and read it often. It reminds me of who I am *in Christ*. They closed their letter with something all Grace Believers should remember. So, I will also close with these same words:

Forgiven in Christ,
Saved in Christ,
Joyful in Christ,
At peace in Christ,
Secure in Christ,
Loved in Christ,
Forever in Christ!

Honoring the *Word of God*,
Dr. David Alan Greene

Other GraceWord Publications

In English

1st Corinthians: Dispensationally Considered

1st & 2nd Thessalonians: Dispensationally Considered

1st & 2nd Timothy & Titus: Dispensationally Considered

2nd Corinthians: Dispensationally Considered

Acts: Dispensationally Considered

Colossians & Philemon: Dispensationally Considered

Ephesians: Dispensationally Considered

Galatians: Dispensationally Considered

Hebrews: Dispensationally Considered

How Am I Wired? Change Begins With Understanding . . .

Philippians: Dispensationally Considered

Romans: Dispensationally Considered

The Glorious Destiny Of Israel – The Fulfillment . . .

The Seven Hebrew Epistles: Dispensationally Considered

Two Distinct Gospel Messages Of The New Testament

En español

Cartas A Teofilo: ¿Estás listo para los últimos tiempos?

El Evangelio Oculto: Una vez fue un misterio pero ahora . . .

Efesios: Dispensacionalmente considerado

The Glorious Destiny Of Israel deals with Scripture as it relates to the children of Abraham. It examines the promises and prophecies God made exclusively to Israel. It sees the Bible solely from a Jewish perspective. These Chosen of God will remain after the Rapture.

The purpose of this book is to present "the other side of the coin." God is faithful and always keeps His promises. The book shows how God will ultimately fulfill these promises and prophecies He made exclusively to Israel.

About The Author

The author has over thirty-five years of experience as an insurance agent managing a multi-state independent agency selling both property and casualty as well as life insurance. During his career, he taught and explained the content and meaning of policies to his clients. Now retired, he continues to devote much of his time to teaching the Bible through rightly dividing the *Word of Truth*.

He obtained his Bachelor of Theology, Master of Biblical Studies, and Ph.D. in Biblical Studies from Evangelical Theological Seminary where he holds the position of Dean of Graduate Studies. He also holds a Ph.D. in Christian Counseling through the National Association of Christian Counselors.

He wrote his dissertation on viewing the Bible from the three systems of theology, those predominantly held by evangelical churches today. Each system yielded a different interpretation. Based upon his research, he published his dissertation entitled

Understanding Scripture – Using the Literary Structure of the New Testament. Now, he presents right division to benefit those who love God and want to understand the Bible both in general and the end times specifically.

Dr. Greene remains committed to following Paul's example. It was Paul who said he was the least of all saints much like the author and many other Christians. However, it is never about us. It is only about Him Who is able to do exceedingly abundantly above all that we ask or think. It is God our Saviour, "Who will have all men to be saved, and to come unto the knowledge of the truth" (1 Tim. 2:4). His Holy Spirit works to accomplish that in each of us.

Paul said that much grace was given to him so that he should preach among the Gentiles the unsearchable riches of Christ. He goes on to say that he wished to make all men see what is the fellowship of the mystery, which from the beginning of the world, had been hidden in God. God reveals to us His Son, the Lord Jesus Christ. It is my desire that you see the fellowship of the mystery where we will forever be *in Christ!*

www.ingramcontent.com/pod-product-compliance
Lightning Source LLC
Chambersburg PA
CBHW060800120626
46557CB00001B/41